DEVINE MAGNETISM AWAKENING THE SOVEREIGN SOUL

Chronicle 29

Panagiota Makaronis

KREA PREA (TM). Est. 2012

Copyright © Janurary 2026 Panagiota Makaronis

All rights reserved

The characters and events portrayed in this book are fictitious. Any similarity to real persons, living or dead, is coincidental and not intended by the author.

No part of this book may be reproduced, or stored in a retrieval system, or transmitted in any form or by any means, electronic, mechanical, photocopying, recording, or otherwise, without express written permission of the publisher.

ISBN: 978-1-7644581-1-5

Cover design by: AI
Editor; KREA PREA (TM). Est. 2012
Written in Australia Victoria Melbourne Craigieburn

I dedicate this to book to those who, have nothing better to do then lie, cheat & screw whom ever to get through.
Happy Hunting

CONTENTS

Title Page	
Copyright	
Dedication	
INTRODUCTION	1
CHAPTER 1	4
CHAPTER 2	13
CHAPTER 3	24
CHAPTER 4	35
CHAPTER 5	46
CHAPTER 6	58
CHAPTER 7	70
CHAPTER 8	82
CHAPTER 9	94
CHAPTER 10	106
About The Author	121
The Theatrical Melodia of my Life : Chronicle On	125
Books By This Author	127

INTRODUCTION

Devine Magnetism: Awakening the Sovereign Soul Chronicle 29.

The continuation to The Theatrical Melodia of my Life. I was back on track stepping onto a new plane of awareness, after hitting a hold up, a knot I needed to break free from. The only way to do so was take a gamble. Only to arrive at a new state of being for the risk I took; has now paid off.

I was to cross a threshold after reaching a crossroad, into a true awakening; only to hit a round up. Here I was again, trying my luck to cancel out that individual I call the rattle snake. He who used me to claim his victory. Returned for another quest, and I was on the other end ready to contest.

I was in and the rest became entertaining, for I hit a downplay. Where I was to begin and where to end that nasty trend, gave me the opportunity to claim my truth. The result was terribly wrong, but, yet again, it was prewritten. By yours truly, to prove my point to give the corrupt a chance to correct.

Rewrite a wrong, a passageway that held me back. For the journey reached its destination, it had me facing an issue, that had been brewing for years. An individual who had been wanting to harm my soul, was watching my success; sitting on my raider insisting he hit me at my best.

That trace was a constant reminder; resilient undeniably

CHAPTER 1

♦ ♦ ♦

IT'S A WITCH HUNT

I was in the mood, to reshape and revalue what I assumed; was part of the gamble. It had me step into the unknown, locked in, warned of what to expect. For what was to come from that outcome, was part of an incur, a kit served well. Handing me an expense that took me by surprise.

It served me a purpose, a well-deserved desire to break the system. It had me feed off the trace where the corrupt saw me easy and forced me to return and follow up on another key. A foundation that changed in a matter of a second that served me a purpose, at the end of that spell.

It forced me through hell; handing me position that took me in. It broke the silence from within. Faced me at every interval, forced to condition the mission, that took me by surprise. It was handing me the evaluation to that manifestation. It forced me off the edge straight into an investigation.

Giving me the indication the impression was nowhere near the imperishable. It was part of a defect that caused an effect. It handed me the evolution to get back on track and resurrect. It gave me an expense that had me forced to hit back with a curse, so I can reverse it to the sender three-fold.

Every thought served me the last resort. It held me up, while the corrupt faced a horrendous trace, at the end of the race. It was part of a trend, that ended and I was handed a key forcing me to replace the old with the new. Emersed with energy, just to cause an effect; before I fail to detest.

It was part of a test that broke the silence. Forcing me to pretend that the game will end, in fact I was put in a position that had me face another proposition. Nothing was stable nor fierce it was all a trace to hand me a case to give me the impression I was taught a valuable lesson.

A challenge that became visible at the end of that trivial pursuit. Had me on the run covering up another final outcome. Where every curse had me rehearse, and every challenge had me come first. It was part of a trace that led me towards the end of the race; trapped in the end of that trend.

In the end it was handing me the entertainment to follow up on another arrangement. A chance that landed me a role, handed me concept that served me well at the end of that ongoing spell. It led me towards a journey that gave me a chance to delve into a trance and trace the corrupt every time.

I hit an avalanche; it had me foreclose a trend, in

the end of that trace. It broke the silence. So, when I reached my peak the energy that served me well then, handed me the honesty I needed to pretend. Giving me the impression every challenge carried a vision to avoid another competition.

Then without earning a point, or leaving it to chance, I had to face another task, from the past. It had me hit a dead-end head on while I remain head strong. It was part of a key, to finalise a challenge, at the end of that trend. Lined me up for a dead end. I had to face a trip down memory lane.

I hit an ending convinced there was no presentation to keep me aligned. It was part of a conscious awareness, it had me facing a truth, making me see every challenge had me on the edge trapped in the middle of a trend. I had been led to believe I hit a dead end; I was taken in and left relentless.

It was in an endless affair, a suffering from within. It gave me a chance to see the end of that trace, facing another case. Bestowing me with a vision to disclaim a collision to that mission; that had me erase every competition. It gave me a second chance to return and evaluate a trace to that fable.

Time was of essence, and I hit a trend, the only thing standing in my way was a dead end. It was part of a trace, it that had me hit a hold up. My freedom was cut short and my light no longer bright. It dimmed just enough light, to have me get through that tunnel. It showed the way; through who.

For everything that had come my way had me facing another bad day. The only tribute that had me troubled in the end; was the one that handed me a dead end. The corrupt entered my realm without words with discrimination just a manifestation that had me facing a reservation.

Another challenge had come by; it gave me a chance to hit back in advance. A trace that served me an emblem at the end of that race. A need to release that beast, it had me follow up on another feast. It was my way, of forcing the corrupt to press replay. I had to face a trace, by causing an effect.

It pushed the corrupt in the corner and faced me with a trace that had me replace another cause an effect. Where in the end it drew me closer just before I hit an encore. With a new trend in mind, I had to find peace, at the end of that feast. When the time come overcome another outcome.

For the frustration that hit me at every destination caused an effect. It gave me a chance to resurrect. All while I took it all in and faced another damn redemption from within. A challenge that hit a holdup it had me face another follow up one that served me well at every warning.

I was to look forward not back, trapped in the middle of a counteract. For those who pushed me off the track, caused an effect and created a deception at the end of that redemption. I had to repeat a retaliation to that manifestation. It was part of retaliation to accompany with a cause an effect.

It had me face the end of that race with a curse I could reverse. All I had to do was come first, face what I thought was the end of the race. While I peruse for a challenge at the end of that step towards a spade. It had me force, that cause of action and override a tradition to that contraption.

A trace to a case that was pending. It had me redeem an

abreaction to that manifestation. It had me back down and face another trace at the end of the race. That is when I knew, the only thing that served me well was the trace that deserted me when I hit royalty.

I hit the end of that trend, that forced me off the edge, straight into a ditch. For that case had me face another trend feeding off the corrupt in the end. I had to face another review, following up on a clue; that had me case close that trace. It forced me off the edge, straight into a lock down.

I was on the edge facing another pledge. Tricked in the middle of a dead end, I had been led on, and left to release that beast, just to give the corrupt a chance to find peace. Forced off the edge just to catch up and trap he who thought he knew me in military as if I was part of his combat.

He assumed he had the industry on his side and I on the edge confiding with the corrupt. They had me conditioning the mission conspiring with another vision. I was forced to hit back with a competition. All so they can pledge, give in and hand me a chaotic event.

Because that assumption became my redemption I got a free ride out of that manifestation. It gave me the chance to fight back in advance. It took me a moment to realise; I was on my own on this one. I made a mistake by giving in, it was handing the corrupt a chance to win.

They were on my raider on a daily basis, watching my every move. Creating a Dynasty around my mission; a test had me forced to protest. The challenge was deceiving; the trace was conniving. In the end every thought that they had was a bluff. They had no freedom; they were way to rough.

It was part of a forethought, that entered my realm when

I was reaching my pinnacle. Where the corrupt had no intention of fighting me. Nor did they have any informative information to hand me an interrogation. The encryption was part of a concept that had nothing to do with me.

It had me conditioning the mission so the corrupt can continue to feed off me. They kept invading in my privacy tormenting me at every belief. That is when I knew someone was on my raider trading up. Trying their luck to catch up; all by feeding off that meeting.

Opening up doors to possibility's that had me wondering; what was my role. Why did they choose me? It made no sense to my reality; it had me on the edge trapped in the middle of an expense. A challenge that served me a wise amount of freedom; a trace that had me face a fierce momentum.

It forced me to hit back with remorse. It had me step into an expense, that served me wonders in the end. The follow up to that mission was based on a comprising composition. Where I had to compromise my mission; catch up and break the corrupts system.

There was no favour to speak of no challenge to redeem. Just a theme to break the silence and the regime a follow up on a trap in between. What they had was my entrance to break that tradition. There association was initiated by the corrupts final resolution, handing me the edge of reason.

Their freedom to create friendships to harm whom ever. Has now become my freedom to drop the bomb, break their system, and feed off that mission. A faith less likely to reprieve, had me step into a challenge that served me wonders. It handed me a key, to face me with brand new reality.

Because the journey was part of a given, it was to help me succeed. The trace that had me face another trend; it pushed me in the corner and forced me to return for a warning. Where every trap had me trick the trend that broke the silence and face another trial in the end.

Given more was not part of that act, it had them parting ways. It handed them an expense that served well at the end of that forthcoming spell. A wizard entered a mastermind who handed them a clue gave them a review and made sure they kept in line so they can get through.

I was taught a lesson left to release, forced to give in. face another trace and follow up on a feast that had me return and find peace. I had to catch up while the corrupt took a moment follow up on a trace. I had to erase, corner he who knew and he who had a clue.

Leading them to a destination, where the concept changed. It caused an effect, handing me a chance to exchange that threat. It turned the journey around to my favour, no longer savouring those who lie to get in, cheat to win. Those who truly have talent fail, the corrupt stir trouble and turn a table.

It became part of a force to be corrupted; by those who were inspired. It served them a treat to that threat that harmed them at the end of that final debt. It handed them a delay to that vision. A singular cycle that made that trend create a follow up on in the end.

Where I was given a trace, to accompany the corrupt at the end of the race. It caused an effect and created a defect broke the silence, trapped me at the end of that trend. I had to repeat, regain conscious awareness again. I was torn in several ways. It created a challenge that had me respite.

I had to heave, then respond, fight back and win every inning; all in one night. It was handing the corrupt a chance to hit back in advance. A given approach where the outcome gave me solidarity. I fell, in a moment of regret, it handed me hell. It led me on straight into a trace; to remain strong.

Forcing me to acclaim another tradition, to a game that had me rewind to the edge facing another trace a given follow up to hand me a vision break the cycle and create a proposition. I was taught a lesson left to release all inhibitions. It led me to a destination that will hand me the reservation.

I was to repeat a presentation, based on a game that took me in. It forced me to face a trial and error. Broadening my horizon and creating a trend that broke the system in the end. I had to take a challenge that had me face reality. A deception to break that precision; an ending to that system.

I had to accompany, what I knew as a feeling not as proof. Then try to collect enough information to put the corrupt at peace. For I was put through, was not a challenge to build character. It was the corrupts way of handing me fear beyond repair so they can have control.

It handed me a proposal to hand me failure all the way. I was taught a lesson based on treason for no reason. It had nothing to do with my character. It is not as if I harmed anyone's peace if they did not harm mine. I minded my own; I kept to myself every which way possible to avoid confrontation.

For those who had nothing better to do but take me in and lead me on. All while they had me face another vendetta.

It forced me to a case that had me release that feast; that shook me when I rose above that hold up. For all I knew there I was heading towards another hardship to that hold up.

For where I was heading, saw me as an easy target. For what they assumed had me feel worse than the motive. Was to hand them the pleasure and the power to repeat and devour. All while they divide and conquer with pressure. Facing me with a curse that had me a return for one more verse.

I was to cause an effect to offer a presentation; mean while hand me a failed validation. It was based on a case that handed the corrupt a chance to lead me on. All while they stalk me in advance, present me with another trance, so when I hit my pinnacle, I could stand to release that feast.

CHAPTER 2

♦ ♦ ♦

HOW TO CATCH A PERPETRATOR

Lock him in, and stir him from within, just to get him to stop pitching in. For I was given a chance to break the cycle in silence. But he who knew had other intentions, it became a part of my journey that me serving them. I was not aware I was being taught a lesson because I had an opinion.

Where my opinion had influence and I never spoke, unless I had something negative to say. For my experiences were depleting the purpose. It had the corrupt plotting to deny me access. For their mission was not what they were expecting. The intension was part of a recission; to break the cycle.

I was on the other end, trapped in the middle of a dead end. Trying my hardest to pretend, that the journey was unacclaimed. I was unable to repeat and start again. For the curse became substantial evidence. It handed me a clue, forced me to hit back with a review, repeat, and replace another clue.

I was accompanied by another review; I took it as good faith. Less likely for me to fail; prevail at every sail. Preventing the corrupt from releasing that trace had me fast forward to next final endeavour. A key trapped me in the middle of a trial and error, a final delay to that dilemma.

I was overlooking the truth, taking the initiative facing a new reality. Feeding off the Holy Grail was my way of sailing through and handing the corrupt a chance to confess. All so I can continue on my journey and disclaim another mission to a game that had me face another bad day.

When I caught up, I could break the corrupts system. Leaving them on the edge starving of affection so I can pledge. They took me in and inverted a new trend at the end of that trace. Assuming each challenge had me cover up a new key. A second chance to delve into a trance and feed off the trace.

The trace became a preparation to the next destination. The corrupt invented a whole lot of lies to serve them a purpose. I lost the evaluation to acclaim another division to that competition. So, when I reached my pinnacle, I could torment the corrupt at every composition, holding them hostage.

It gave me a chance to redeem myself; used abused. Left to witness a whole lot of bad news. The journey became genocide and the only way out was to cause an effect. Create a demonic tread, feed off the system, and start fresh. Finalising that energy that had me regain conscious awareness again.

I had to face another vision to that proposal; it had me return to discard another event. The one that had me follow up on a clue, giving me the impression every trace had a revelation. It was causing an effect and handing me an evolution that restored my energy and faced me with a debt.

All while I raid those who raided me in the head. Leading them to a destination with dead ends and death threats. There was no reservation to speak of, for that commune turned into revenue. leaving them suffering in silence so I can get through. Repeating a trend at the end of that dead end.

I was given an ulterior motive, left to release that beast that forced me off the edge. Waiting for the curse to reverse, had given me an allegation; to reach that preservation. It had me causing an effect letting the law of gravity to take effect. A new faith that had me forced to hit back with an uproar.

A reservation had been preserved for another hit. It took me on journey, that was torn, and once again; I had been taken for granted. Meanwhile the energy that forced me off the edge faced me with a brand-new karmic effect. I was haunted by the past, living in the present and trying my best to make do.

For what I was handed, claimed its truth. It was part of a clue that will force the corrupt to take that challenge and break the system at every point of view. Where I was given a reason to hit back with treason and a challenge that will serve me well and break the silence while I went through hell.

At the end of the that trace, it landed me role. It was part of a gift that will serve me well and whole. It handed me a disgrace that served me an allegation. It forced me to release that beast at every destination. It gave me a chance to elevate, while I take that trend, towards the next level.

An ending to that battle, was unbeatable. For the challenge to come first, had me face another case. I fell head over heels, trying to investigate another follow up; to the next round up. For it was each to their own and I was on the cusp of creating a challenge that had me face another corrupt.

It had me tracing another force to that cause. It was giving me the impression the light at the end of the tunnel was just another way of accepting defeat along the way. There was reminder to that decipher. Just a kind heart that handed me the impression; I hit a hard condition to that mission.

It was leaving me to investigate, interrogate and follow up on another release to that feast. it forced me off the edge straight into a destination that had me follow up on another investigation. I had to release that beast that forced me to repeat a trace to that case.

It had me on the move, terribly wrong, because I was tied up all along. Left to undo release, then try to find peace from all that abuse that had me waste valuable energy trying to erase what I thought was the last resort. It had me question the motivation of those who knew.

Whatever possessed them to face me with a lie, handed me conclusion; to get by. The assumption brought me back to salvation. For the thought of harming me now will backfire right through. It caused an effect handed out a final. Purely to take the initiative and place the corrupt in lockdown.

All so I can continue on my path, with no trace nor trend

to fail me in the end. It was part of a given momentum that had me facing another trip down memory lane. It was to help me see the light and fight off another demon that forced me off the edge straight onto the narrow. Hitting ground zero.

It caused an effect, that had me release that beast. It had me determine who when and where the drama began. I had to follow up on a case that had me face the end of that trend. It brought me forward back to reality again. I had to divide conquer and follow up on another drama.

I had to claim my truth in the end of that trend. It had me face a true reality; towards a destination that took me on journey that faced me with a final reservation. A given reason to hit back with treason. It had me on the edge impersonating a pledge imperishable to that title.

A mission that handed me a competition. Took me on a pathway that handed me the truth, it faced me with an enigma that presented me with a lie. It took me on a journey that served me well and forced me to get by, on a forthcoming event. It instilled what I thought was the last resort.

It took me on a journey that restored my energy; fed me a final lie. Just to give the corrupt a chance to belt me in advance. They stalled, long enough to see the truth unfold; only to realize the journey was put on hold. Everyone who was in on it; found a way out. Harm me and hand me doubt.

A chance to see my world evolve, had me on the edge of reason. Waiting for the corrupt to gang up on me, repeat a treason, a trace for no reason. It had me on the edge, raided in the head by the culprit who assumed he had energy to consume. The corrupts second coming, was part of a trick.

It was over raided and understated. I had to state a fact, face a trace, catch a break, and pretend I never knew. In the end I fell into a mission, that had me break the aurora to that proposition. My aura changed and the energy that followed had me face a trace and trap those who contemplate.

I fell into a trap that had me validated with a consummation to hand the corrupt a chance to violate that tradition that gave me a vision and handed me a proposal that served me well and gave me a second chance to get back on track and face another impact at the end of that trend.

It had me pretending everything was pending. I was not part of that race; I was part of a bigger picture. The tension had me on the edge redeeming another reasoning. It gave me a chance to hit back in advance, reminding me the only thing that took me in; was the drama the served me well.

I had release to give the corrupt a chance to find peace. I can follow up on a feast at the end of that trace that forced me to give in and replace another case. I had to embrace another extension to that redemption cause an effect repeat and resurrect all in one setting.

Eventually I was drained left to remain silent to the game. I could not repeat nor remain the same and the only thing that had me face another case was the drama that forced me to get in and win another inning. It had me on the move trapped in the middle of a competition.

It was a given a trace that was part of a given, a challenge that had me face the forbidden. I had to feed off the dream override it in-between. I was given an opportunity to release that demon that forced me to repeat and report that trace that had me face another case.

It handed me a demonic energy, facing that demon and winning every truth. What I had to go through to catch up and catch a break was unbelievably uncanny. It had me step into the unknown creating a war a follow up on a feast to give the corrupt a chance to return for an encore.

I had to advance and break the system. I had to trace it, chase away he who returned to steal another key. I had to overcome it and look forward to another summit. It had me on the move returning one more groove. It was part of a challenge to cut the corrupt short.

I had leave them hunting for more asking for war. That is when I knew I hit the forthcoming review. I was looking ahead with a positive outlook, overlooking the truth. Looking for answers, all while the corrupt hit me with dirty glances. I was taught a lesson, left to erase that case.

All while I cause an effect and create an extension to that redemption, preaching my truth. In the end of that trend the method hit a dead end. It was leaving me warned of that conspiracy in the end. I was enslaved in a trap that had me forsake another trend in the end.

I hit a final, an expense with denial, it was part of an extremely hard truth. It had me facing another trace giving into the corrupt so can catch up and preparing me for a truth. All so I can give in and feed off that trace from within. I had to look ahead force my way through just to get ahead.

It had me stepping into the unknown, facing another warning. All so the corrupt can continue to grow. I had to heave hold up to the next breed, feeding off the foundation that had me start fresh. I had to break the silence and cycle. Where every follow up had me returning for another trivia.

It had me on the edge pretending that every case had me follow up on another trend. It was part of revival that had me face a trace that had me trapped in the middle of a riddle. I had to step into a position worse than the mission. I was facing another trial, forced to hit back with denial.

So, when I hit the end, the only thing holding me back was the trace to that energy that had me back on track. I had to face another force to cause an effect, stating the obvious. It served me well and took me on a journey from heaven to hell. I was held in contempt forced to claim a train of thought.

An indicative approach that had me initiating the truth. It forced me to hit back and break the cycle. It had me get back on track, following up on a journey that served me well. Even though I had nothing to show. It still remained instilled in my mind handing me an Omen.

It served the corrupt the willingness to return for another feast. A follow up to that tradition that handed me a competition. I had to release, all while I was going through hell. I was given a tradition that served me well; it threw me off the raider, straight into hell.

I was taught a lesson, trapped in the middle of a trace. It had my head undo another case. I was passing test and the corrupt were following me waiting for me to fail while they swerve to next recreational endeavour a journey like no other. It served me well and had me reach my potential.

All while I continue to face a trace, reaping a reward and facing the truth. It had me causing an effect a meaningful one just to help me get back on the road to recovery. It had me face a trend that had me forced to start again. It held me up and help me get ahead.

A royalty to that dynasty had created contract, it was to serve me another ammunition. It served me a wonder and forced me redo acclaim and return for a brand-new spanking clue. It was part of a thread of redemption in the end of that placement. I was handed a clue forced to face the facts.

All so I can skip that too, forcing me to repeat rebel and put the corrupt through hell. Just so I can find peace after that feast. It was handing me the resurrection to that manifestation that will claim another vision to that mission. Handing me a competition to that composition.

Every journey I was on was too harsh to harm me. I was given a degree of challenges that served me. Every time I found my way through, it gave me a second chance to delve into a trance. Reminding me, I had to face another trace, condition the mission, and follow up on another vision.

The only thing that broke the silence; was the last thing that harmed me from within. Where it had me face a trace at the end of the case. Where I was given an opportunity to rise above that unity. I entered a realm that was incoming and ingoing, it had me facing another trace to that case.

I had to follow up on a given, a trend that handed the corrupt a dead end. All so I can continue to break the silence and repeat another trace at the end of the race. It had me face another internal investigation. Challenge those who knew, a task that was inconclusive to he who knew.

Let those who had a clue in, purely to see I was innocent from within. Here I am back again; with the same bright outlook the one that had me facing another entranced to a foundation that left repeating an old wound and the corrupt waiting to see where they can return and steal another key.

I had to repeat it and harm the key that I earned periodically; again, with a united front in the end. There was no disconnection, it was part of a failed presentation, to that manifestation. I had to cancel the energy, cave in on the case. It had me consecrate, those who were wrong all along.

For an entourage to that encore had laid me to rest caused an effect and let me down. It had me cave in on the concept and led me to believe the crown was not mine to begin with. It was a curse I could reverse unless I rehearsed it giving the corrupt a chance to see what the plan will be.

All so they can return to harm me, forcing me to fight back with scrutiny. For he who harmed me had me was on the edge, leading the pact. Leaving me disguised; a road that trapped me in the end of that abode. When I looked within; a journey that served me well; was the one that took me in.

It put me through hell, trapped me with a certain degree of challenges; I could not deal with. I was put on a journey that did not suit me. It had me stepping into a dead end, facing the corrupt in the end of that trend. For the trace was imperishable. It was to keep me in touch with the corrupt.

Just to hand them a chance to hit back in advance. I had to face an extension to that redemption. It forced me to fight back and follow through to a destination that had me redeem scheme and hit back with a follow up on another theme. Hide to attempt once again to harm me with interrogation.

I had to compromise and follow up on a new fleet. Then catch the corrupt before they attempted to return and hit me with a new improved journey in-between. It had me praising the demon that served me a death threat. Because I was too busy fighting in combat, with the demon from within.

There was something untrue about that trace, it served me a rock that was kindly stating a fact. It brought me forward and led me toward a trend; that broke the silence in the end. I was on the prowl trying my hardest to harvest. For he who knew wanted to face me a repeat something new.

That is when I knew I hit an entrance to the unknown; unwelcome. It had me opening the wrong doors I assumed but in fact those who knew wanted to harm me right through. All by hitting me with hate all because Love wanted to screw me right through.

Where the honest opinion took me on a journey that had me on the edge repeating a threat. Trapped in the middle of a riddle, trying my luck repeating another bad luck. I had to focus and create a new feast to that piece reminiscing again from an imperishable a release to that feast.

CHAPTER 3

◆ ◆ ◆

TIME TO EMBRACE THE TRUTH

> *I was torn in more than one direction, leading the pact towards a journey of resurrection. It had me laughing at myself way too much I could not see the reality. For what it was worth and what was to come from that outcome; was part of an expense; that had me second guessing.*

I was causing effects, living a lie. I do not fail and lose my life before I make my mark. The decision to leave me facing a competition, was based on a case. I on the edge repeating a failed mission. I was brought on this earth to bring forth peace; and the earth-bound spirits turned into feast.

For those who knew and those who had a clue, thought ending my life sooner. It will bring forth an energy that will serve them well and hand me a dead end so they can continue to grow forcing me to out claim and follow up on another game. All so they get in and gain wisdom from within.

I had to foreclose an enclosed event that had me manifesting into another debt. It had me facing a reservation to that manifestation. It was my way of accepting a defined it was to come first and ever so fast. It had me repeat and follow up on another trace at the end of the race.

I had to state a fact clear the air cleanse my spirit and look forward to another truth and dare. Where the last resort had me undo that final review. Just to enter realm that had me forced to hit back somehow. So, when I reached that peak the clean way out will be the drama, I set free.

All so the corrupt can continue to feed off me. It had me state a fact, trace that trap and give into those who harmed me from within. I had to face a fear, just to get back on track and feed off the trace that had me look forward and face me at the end of the race.

I was taught a lesson left to trace a trap give in to those who caught up and had me face them as if the corrupt were more powerful than I. Giving me the impression to hand me a key and hand me the foundation to create a better entrance a trace that had me face another case.

Unless I was served well and given an opportunity to delve into a trace. There was a portion to that notion, that handed me a potion. In case I had to catch up and feed off the trend that brought me forward in the end. It handed me a desired disgrace, to that trace.

Served well when I took the first step into hell. I was taken by surprise; it took me in facing another win. It had me face and force my way through delegating and avoiding another

25

allegation to that scrutiny that left those rumours on hold. It had me face another trace at the end of the case.

I had no respite; I was full of spite, for those who knew were hunters. Hired by unforeseen source to give me a moment to survive another dive. Before they entered an aim at my feet, then try their luck to press delete. They gave me a worry, and in turn debated what to do to break my system.

I was to end that saga with a journey like no other. Catch he who was stalking me; in the end, hoping that the trace will start and I will give in handing the corrupt a dead end in the end of that win. I hit a trial that served me well at the end of that trend it forced me to pretend.

I was to get ahead. Sending subliminal messages to those who forced their way in. It had me face another trial a trace and a trap that had me give in and feed off the win. It gave me the passion and the trend that forced me to reach my potential. It led me to believe that the worst was in front.

The words I use were powerful; it gave that demon a chance to speak his mind. It had me on the edge warned once again. Attempting to put me in my place so he can win a fight. Leading me to destination and I could redo acclaim and face a new game.

It had me facing a reason to hit back with treason. But I was trying to fight back, by giving in and getting back on track it had me face another trace so the corrupt can undo another clue. I had to force my way in accompanying me to come forth and feed of the corrupt from within.

in the end of that final feast, I was given a chance to release peace get back on track and face another impact. It was serving me well and presenting me with a key that saved me. In the end of that forthcoming spell. An error from within was stabilizing that truth. It had me face a truce.

A trial in the end of that trend became final I had no faith not trend no challenge and no trick to defend my honour in the end. Feeding of the concept so I can release and find peace preparing my soul for one more chance to beat the corrupt to the punch. A trend that served me well.

Where the only way in was create a challenge that had me on the edge restoring my energy and starting again. If I case close keep up with the program trouble the corrupt with a chance to hit back in advance. It will give me a chance to overtake and create a challenge to solve another issue.

I caught him in the act and spoke my truth; God help me know there is Hell to pay. All because that Demon had no freedom what he had was a motive the one I gave him because he created that piece and I gave in on the condition I feed off that feast. It will give me a sentence that will save me.

I was given a chance to hit back in advance at the end of that trace. It handed me travesty a trail an error and final vendetta. To give the corrupt a presentation that had me finalising a reservation. I was to manifest a challenge that saw me easy giving me the role to return and face an impact.

The soul intervened and saw me face another trace at the end of that case. It caused an effect and broke the system at the end of that tradition. I had to beat the buzzer follow up on another reasonable doubt. So, when I reached my peak the only thing that had me standing; relapsed.

They had trapped me in the middle of a curse; I could not reverse. Because the journey served me well. It took me in and saved me from trapping he who knew and creating a concept to skip me right through. It was the last thing that took me in and the first thing that threw me out from within

I had to give in, challenge that method from within. For every momentum had me certain that the trace was uncanny. The trend was unravelled and the only thing that had me switched was the entrance to a tremor that forced me through hell. Straight into a dilemma that had me face a finally.

I was on the edge, trapped in the middle of a pledge. It was part of a presentation, that warned me I was way out of line. In the end of that validation, it gave me a chance to hit back in advance. It was a part of a reach to rise above and beyond what I thought was out of reach.

In fact, it was just about to be breached. I felt trapped out of bounds a trend that hit a hold up in the end. It was my way of getting through reaching my limit was pointless because I hit a free ride to the other side wondering what I did to release that beast; that forced me to find peace.

All so the corrupt can condition the mission and feed off that trend that served me well in the end. It had me on the edge, teaching the corrupt a valuable lesson. All while I give in and serve them a pause and effect from within. A follow up on a journey that served me well; prepared me for hell.

A test of endurance that put me through the abys. Had served its purpose, it led me towards a journey of repetition. A united front with those who had the energy to release that beast. It forced me off the edge handing me power to undo, devour. Serving me a setting of a siren and a beheading.

A legacy that stood its ground in time of need, had a

purpose. For the power to fight back had me faced with a review. An overview, leading me to a destination that started a fight and had me reach my potential to claim my truth. I had to face a case to that trace that warned me I hit a dead end.

The energy that took its toll had repeated a new roll. It forced its way in finalising what I thought was an evaluation to that manifestation it had me reaching my potential; way to early. I was on edge restoring my energy feeding off the synergy that had me face a review at the end of that scheme.

It had them forced to revive another faith to that trend that created a dead end. Every reservation was causing an effect. Handing me a lead so I can resurrect, leading me towards a journey of love, hate, then towards rejuvenation. Meanwhile, make sure I never lose my will power to succeed.

The trend that served me well in the end. Gave me a second chance to pretend, handing me the trace to serve me a feast at the end of the race. It forced me through hell creating an extension to that redemption forcing me to hit back and feed off that reception.

The lesson was lessened, and lenient. The trace was based on condition that was part of an evil investigation. Where the corrupt had their view and decided to return for an overview. I did not know how to fight back nor even attempt a trip down memory lane; to get back on track.

It was saving the corrupt down the track. Giving me the impression I had no reservation; just a constant reminder I was left feeding off the interrogation. It had me facing what I thought will bring forth peace, in fact it was a trace that had me finalising the energy that was returning for a yearning.

An indicator from a past faith; had me realise I was unforgiven. I was taught a lesson, left to return with a final leap of faith. A lead that had me succeed; it was part of a test that had me raid the heads of those who wanted to look forward try their luck get back on track by feeding off the corrupt.

A trap had challenged had me to find an avenue to save me. I had to succeed feeding off the trend that had me hit a dead end. An energy that led me to release that beast that forced me to repeat facing another trace at the end of the race. It was part of a key that will hand me a final unity.

I was on the edge; I had no rope to hang on to and no hope to stand my truth. The myth becomes part of a trace that had me foreclose another case at the end of the race. My ground was unprecedented and the energy that had me profound; served me well.

So, when they needed to get through hell. They presented me with a challenge that took me on a passageway, forcing me to press replay. It was part of a trend that had me face a feast; forcing me to release and find peace. I was on the move, after the fact; caught up in a web of lies just.

Stepping into the unknown was a challenge. It had me hit the end of that trend releasing that demon that had me start again. Just to get back on track and create a safety net. Handing the corrupt a dead end at the end of that trend. Forcing me to release that demon and start again.

For they were hitting me periodically, facing me with a key and a concealer to repeat another feast to that beast that had me face a trace at the end of the case. It was cancelling every challenge. It led the corrupt towards a journey that had me follow up on trace conditioning the mission.

For what I thought was a final degree, gave me a second chance to hit back in advance. Every time I hit an ending the energy that presented me with a clue. It had me facing a dead end, restoring my faith in humanity again. Preventing the corrupt from starting new trend was my way through.

I had to follow up on a key, feeding off the mission. Presenting the corrupt with a final admission. Admiring every concept, lined me up for a key that had me face another force to that final degree. It caused an effect an extension to that redemption that had me face another competition.

It gave me a chance to hit back with remorse. I was on the mend, ready to hit back with a brand-new trend. A follow up on a review, just so I can start again. It had me feeding off the energy that handed me a curse I could reverse because I was branded.

Stalling long enough to release that beast that had me face another feast. Because I could sense something sinister coming my way the energy that had me press replay caused an effect and faced me with an energy that had me resurrect. Even though the journey was interrogating me.

I had to face a trace an embarrassing momentum to that trend had me on the edge repeating another system in the end. It was a kind way of belting the corrupt all the way. Where the only thing that come my way had me releasing a bad day. A challenge that was worth its weight in gold.

I was served a trace that had me face another case. Attempting to deny me access at the end of the race. I was on the move hitting a challenge, that had me face another curse to reverse. For the right to sit back and create an endangered event had me trapped in the end of that dead end.

with a new avenue on my radar. Admired by the concept, leaving it to chance; partly at a given glance a reminder that the corrupt wee on my raider instigating another fight at the end of that trend that had me repeat and report what I thought was the last resort.

I was handed a challenge that created a review. No longer part of a maintained event. It was part of a presentation to hand the corrupt a resignation just to face an investigation. A task to make room for improvement had come to fruition. I was given an opportunity to relive repeat a past event.

An allegation that served me well, gave me a chance to prove my innocence in advance. It was presenting me with a challenge to catch up, finalise the mission and feed off the competition. It handed me a chance to repeat an old game; that had me gambling my dream away.

I was put through hell trapped in the middle of a spell. Where this time around the method was profound. I reached my pinnacle beyond physical belief and the expectation that took a challenge that had me reach my peak. Threatening those who knew and feeding off those who had a clue.

Meanwhile force the corrupt off the edge straight into a disloyal pledge. Giving them the impression the only salvation to that manifestation was the one that had me case that dead end feeding off the trace that served me well in the end. It was left to the imagination; every chance caused an effect.

It was handing me an ending that served me well. Presenting me with a curse the put me through hell. I was on the edge, returning for an ending that will bring me forth, a challenge. One that will serve me well handing me the influence I need to get through hell.

For the one thing that had me survive was the last thing standing. It had me reach my peak break the cycle create a distance between he who knew and he had a clue. It was forcing me to reach the end of that passageway. It had me waiting for the corrupt to face another trace.

I had to repeat, line the corrupt up for a new treat. For what I thought was part of a task, had me face another trace at the end of the race. I had to go back and forth reminiscing a past event. It had me state a fact after the fact, face another rising to that conviction then hold me to ransom.

So, when I reach my pinnacle the statement will meet its quota, and the trace will break the cycle. It was handing me an evaluation to the next destination and an extension to that transformation. It paused an effect and created a redemption at the end of that deception.

For that reason, I was given a chance to hit back in advance. It presented the corrupt a dead end at the end of that trace. It had me give in and finalise that redemption to that trial that caused an effect it handed me the resolution to get back on track and feed off the trap that served me well.

It handed me a forthcoming spell the one that will hand me that everlasting investigation to that manifestation. where the truth come out and I could replace it with an energy that was serving me well it was feeding off the threat clear the debt and finalise that truth that had me on the edge.

I was unreasonably attacked, left to return the favour

before I could break that chain. A task that was harming me spirit in the end of the game. It was part of a journey I could pledge, and a key that had me face another reservation to the next destination.

Then when the time come create a challenge, and a trace that had me facing another trend in the end. It was Pushing the corrupt in the corner hitting them with a dead end. A challenge that will serve me well and face me while I hit the end of that forthcoming spell that served me well.

I saw the ending pending, it gave me a chance to dive into a second trial. I had to feed off the trace that had me erase the case. It was part of a challenge, that had me embrace the truth. Feed off the key, create a piece, and remind me, I had more power to undo and less than a minute to review.

CHAPTER 4

◆ ◆ ◆

I HAD TO FOLLOW UP & FACE THE FACTS ONCE MORE

It had me following up on a case that was closed. Delving into a challenge that served me well. It was giving me the impression I hit an extension to that manifestation that had me alter another condition to that mission. Redeeming every follow up to the next exhibition, the final decision.

It had me locked in overlooking the truth, so when I caught up, I could undo that clue. I had to free myself from the corrupt, waiting, and accepting defeat. It had contemplating what to do next and how to cave in on the mission from within. It caused an effect, trapped in the middle of that debt.

For the corrupt were to return and belt me from within.

It forced me to redo acclaim and face another train of thought, so I can catch up and feed off the corrupt. It was part of a trend that had me forced to return and fight for the truth in the end. For those who knew had me return.

They created a war in my peace, forcing me to declare innocence once more. They had me perform on a platform, in a dream that caused an effect. I had to redeem another theme to that scheme. I had to follow up on a presentation, that had me feed off the interrogation, breaking the system.

The urge to reclaim what I assumed was the end of that commune. It had become a challenge in the long run, for another allegation to the game had me think twice. A given reason to hit back with treason, what had come to fruition had come to my attention.

I had to trap those who knew and create a war in my peace with those who had a clue. All so I can catch up get through and prepare myself for another review. All while I get in and feed off the drama from within. Because I was taken advantage of it had me in admin, overriding that test.

It had me request another contest, all while the rest fed off the quest. It had me condition the mission delving into a world of my own. Forcing me to hit back and face another wind up, a turnkey handing me the evaluation all while I get back on track and feed off the presentation.

It handed me an evaluation, based on a condition that served me well. It had me face an awareness that took me on a journey that led me to believe that the worst was behind me. For every drama and every dream, had me fight back and create an anomaly in-between.

For every concept that served me, well had me presenting

the corrupt a with a final spell. I was on the move warned of what was to come from that outcome. It was part of a trip down memory lane. It had me break every thought and handed me a way of that doubt.

Where every trial caused an effect and took me on a journey to help me resurrect. I was taken by surprise left to reminisce, fooled by the foolish just to feed off the trace that had me forced to walk out of that debt without doubt. I was losing myself worth as I released that beast.

It forced me to rely on the corrupts feast, a method to get by. All while handing me a key that had me face another degree. Where my intuition took over the mission and in the end of that competition, I was given a chance to release that beast that had me face another feast.

It was part of an enigma, where that proposition landed me a role. I was trapped in the end of that trend, tracing someone's dead end. There were several close up and personal, trying their luck predicting future events. I played it purely to feed off the debts and the death threats.

Dictating my every move, trying to catch up and then attempt to take the initiative and try my luck to feed off the corrupt again. All by latching on to me, handing me bad luck. Assuming I will be fighting a lost cause a dead end to that battle. I was ticked off and trapped in the middle of a riddle.

A wall that collapsed and had me see, I was nowhere near the corrupts predictability. In fact, I was caught up in an act of kindness, attempting to break that cycle in the end. I was put in a position less likely for me to predict and more likely for me to detain another vendetta to the game.

It had me gambling my truth away, a challenge that led

me it on. It led me to believe that every trace brought me forward and forced me to embrace the broader picture. Where I get to order the trend feed off the trace break the system forced my way in and face another prediction from within.

It was part of another key serving me well and presenting me with a challenge that had me state the obvious and that was I had no trace, what I had was the end of that case a prediction that led me to an investigation that locked me in and fed off me from within.

It was all based on a cover up; it had me face another internal presentation. Feeding off the concept that was breaking the cycle and limitation to that interrogation. All while I give in and face another prediction from within. The act of extending the warranty was challenging me.

I was taught lesson, left to embrace that trace. It had me enlightened with a tale; an untold story that needed to prevail. Before I was to enter the new, a realm to create a piece at the end of that final release. It had me tread for a new improved debt. A challenge that had me face another threat.

A deity that had me face a tremor at the end of that vendetta. One gamble after the next feeding of the release so I can pay out another debt. A threat that gave me the impression there was no allegation it was part of an investigation that served me well; literally put the corrupt through hell.

I found myself tied up in a web of lies, the only way I could redo was interrogate those who knew. Then feed off the edge of reason all while I gang up on those who had a clue. I had to follow up on a clue. Trapping those who wonder off and create a trap at the end of the race.

The corrupt were returning to manipulate and interrogate me. It had me manifesting another dream, one that was meant to become a nightmare in-between. It became a fight and I ended in a battlefield a warrior. It was part of a chance to belt them with a trance in advance.

It handed the corrupt sheer silence, and I a chance to renew and follow up on justice. Because the corrupt saw me easy, they thought they could stalk me; then influence my thoughts. A trace that served me well at the end of the race. For the curse was to reverse and I was to come first and last.

Little did they know, the little white lie was based on my thoughts. I had to lure them in and face another trace, giving the corrupt a chance to erase. It had me face what I thought was about to encourage me to begin a new trap to that trend that handed me a dead end.

I was given a chance to return and feed off the forbidden. A case that caused an effect and presented me with a chance; to delay that defect. It was hitting me with a final frontier. Where I get in and define that defect; it took me on journey towards a restoration from that manifestation.

I was yearning for a good time, a moment where I can put all my woes and enemies aside. So, when I reach my pinnacle, I can enter that realm, that hit back with a trace that had me face another case. A given momentum to release that beast that forced me to repeat reclaim and press delete.

I had to get back on track and feed off the impact, a given trend. A forbidden energy that failed me in the end. It was holding on to me and the forte for way to long that is when I knew I hit another final review. Hoping I would give in and face another tremor from within.

All while the corrupt were faking, an expansion to that redemption. For what I thought was the last resort, had me on the edge presenting the corrupt with a threat and a dead in the end. I was to give in and pretend that the trace was no longer part of that case; that was pending.

An event that was delayed, caved in on me. It gave me a second chance, to divide and conquer another wrong move. It was leading me to a destination where I was given a chance to face another curse and rehearse, a feast to that piece. It handed me the incur to return for encore.

I was given a reason to hit back with treason. Taught a lesson, give in, feed off the energy that had me face, trinity from within. Just to see it all unfold, as if I was the reason the world fell into a catastrophe. I was part of a war, living proof, unaware I was being stalked on the purpose arch up.

Struggling like the rest in, the west, north and southeast, a challenge that had me on the edge. I was reaching my pinnacle and feeding off the trend that had me face and hit a dead end. As if I was to blame and only, I should be living in shame. Because it was part of a game changer.

Where it handed me a release, to face another feast. Fight back a losing battle, just to help me get back on track and feed of that rattle. It had me raid that test feed off that conquest and present the corrupt with a burn. A final challenge that will help me survive another dive.

A presentation to wind down from that limitation was irritating me. It was part of an irregular beat, trapped in the middle of a riddle. An imitation formed by a key that had me face another final degree. A challenge that manifested, had given me the impression I had no reason to hit back.

All I had was treason. Trapped in the middle of a feast, waiting to save solve then surrender all while I unfold. Leading me towards a challenge that caused an effect and handed me the evolution to break the system. I no longer was holding on to a cycle that was holding me hostage.

The events that had me reach my vision, caused an effect, and fed off the composition. The corrupt were ready; willing to plead guilty. I had them locked in, awaiting patiently, to be served waiting to begin a new improved inning. An ending that was pending and a challenge that was never ending.

I had enough information to lead me towards a journey that had me reach my potential. It created a follow up to another divination that will stand its ground and create a follow up towards a trace that will serve me well at the end of the race. I had to divide conquer and feed off the vision.

It had me in admin, waiting for the corrupt to return for a competition. It handed me an invasion to an inspection that led me towards a journey that forced me to redo a follow up. I was on review, those who knew saw me as an easy target. The only method they had was to hit back with treason.

The challenge was to change them entirely, handing out the cold hard truth. I had no freedom to revive, no interim to get back on track either. I was to survive on a method with no trace to condition the mission just a reasonable doubt to reclaim revive and follow up on another dive.

I had to give in because I was influenced by spirit to face another trace. For the corrupt were way too easy, they were on my raider watching my every move. Looking over their shoulder, waiting for me to show up so they can fail me. But all it did was hand me key and feed off their journey.

It was to give me a curse I cannot reverse, a challenge to allow me in, handing me a chance to win. For the method was too hard to hide and the journey became final. That is when I knew I was no longer having to live in denial. It was giving me the impression; the chase was not based on envy.

It was part of a bigger picture a journey that will take me further. The corrupt were overlooking every task, looking for answer. They assumed stalking me and stealing the combination key, will rectify every sanctity to their evangelical vampire effects. It had me on the edge facing a pledge.

Breaking the system and starting again had me face another predicament in the end. I had to feed off the tremor and forfeit another dilemma. So, when I hit that pinnacle the only thing standing was the last thing that had me face another tremor from that terror, a challenge like no other.

It will give me the impression I can redo and follow up on another review. It forced me to state the obvious a trend that had me face a dead end. The fact it had me fall into a trap and prepare me for a key that served me well intuitively. I tended to catch up and then hit a hold up because of it.

The trend was trending leading me on. It was forcing me to fight for my life, double time; just to remain strong. It served me well in the end of that spell and even though the proof was weak the end was blunt and I fell into a heap. A trace that was pending at the end of the race caved in on me.

Because the journey ended in tragedy it had me hitting back at the last minute. It saved me just at the nick of time, because I hit the finish line. I was left to hold to an old belief, that was meant to be left behind. But the new year became frivolous to those who needed my help.

The decision to make me pay for their wrongdoing, was part of a deviation, to their manifestation. They were instigating a fight and investing in it to hoping they will win a bet and fail me right through. It had me facing another trend, feeding off the complexity in the end.

It had me forced to repeat and rebel against those who took me in. It had me face a trace to hand me a new beginning. It had me facing an abreaction, from a part manifestation. Where they decided to create war in my piece. There were several in on it and none were admitting the truth.

Time to create a piece, catch them in the act then when the time come; cause an effect. It had me break the system, where the corrupts mission to sabotage me; now backfired. Not only do they have a dead-end, a death threat to undertake but they put me through hell, for a long-term effect.

Assuming that the method they used against me will break me. Leaving me scrapping for air hitting the earth, dry reaching from the dry heat. But all it did was create a challenge that had me trying to catch up from the corrupts lie. All so they can miscommunicate; the challenge to help me get by.

I fell into a trap a given momentum to get back on track. It was based on a case that forced me to repeat. It gave me a chance to hit back in advance and follow up on a journey that had me repeat another yearning to that theme. The one that forced me to hit back in-between.

I had to feed off the trace a follow up on a past event. Served well, while breaking the system, and putting those who were part of it through hell. I was on a journey worse than imagined. For that journey was torn and the trace was risen by the tradition that had me face another competition.

The energy that had me refine and face another crime, took me in. I had to fight my way through while those who knew could not wait to face me and repeat after the fact. Breaking the cycle and pushing me off track. For that first and last result had me facing another trial to that trend.

It had me forced to hit back with a dead end. They tried their luck to harm me with a final review. facing the corrupt to resume another clue. For they assumed I was lady luck. If anything, my experience so far has been nothing but unfair, unfaithful to the point of no return.

I had no luck where the corrupt were involved, there were way too many magots; to speak of. Those who knew, those who had a clue created a piece to stop me from repeating, clearing the air. It had me on the edge, denying them access while I delete delay; put them back where they started.

They took me in and decided what my destiny should be like. Leaving me suffering silence while they continued to roam laughing at me as if I deserved to live in a desirable effect. In fact, I was a victim to scrutiny. To the point I hit their unity, leaving them surviving turning against each other.

Breaking the chain had the system trapped once again. For the trace and the case was making sure the journey was serving me an encore. I had to give in and change my destiny from within; a feast to release the beast. Giving me the impression I hit a resolution, a distinction; that served me well.

I was given a chance to hit back in advance. Troubling the corrupt and facing another trial an error. It had me on the edge hitting the corrupt with a final vendetta. Where in the end of that spell, I was given a chance to hit back in advance. Presenting them with a challenge that cannot be outspoken.

It was tormenting them, leaving them testing my patience. Assuming I was forced to return and repeat another turn. In fact, it was part of the journey, there was unfinished business. Karmic effect if you will, where the corrupt were covering up a reel, to that skill; that had me forced to reveal.

It was handing me a chance to clear my road; feed off the energy and the abode. It served me a willingness to return, feed off the breed unleash a seed. Trapped me in the end of that trend a momentum to pretend. I had to face a trace to get back on track forcing the corrupt to confess.

CHAPTER 5

◆ ◆ ◆

THE RETURN OF THE GUARDIAN, OF PEACE & JUSTICE

> *I was taught a lesson, tempted fate with the guardian of Peace and justice; just to catch a break. A commandment that was part of an interim, to that method that forced me to release redo and acclaim another clue. It had me in terrible shape, facing another conspiracy at the end of the race.*

An internal investigation gave me a second chance, to hit the corrupt with an interrogation. I was on the edge, torn into shreds, I had to go through it all. Meanwhile trying my hardest to harvest while the corrupts failure to reach me gave me a chance to give in an indication, I won another enquiry.

A step into the right direction, forced me to hit the corrupt with a final feast. A foundation that served me well at the end of that release. Where the corrupt loose resurrection and I get back on track feeding off the manifestation. It had me reaching my pinnacle with no lack of reservation.

It was part of a story untold, a trace unfolding to hand me a traditional effect. A need for resurrection from that validation that served me wrong move. It was a made-up story in my head that handed me the energy I needed to get ahead. I was on the edge warned me of the possibilities.

It had me face a royal flush, hitting back with pride and prejudice, no debt nor death threat. It gave in and handed me a final revenue. A chance to hit back with a first and last never-ending cast. A list so huge I lost my will to release and my foundation to find peace.

I had to undo that clue and face another revue. It warned me I was way too harsh trying my hardest to harvest while the rest were no longer in the middle of a quest it was part of a given and a foundation to release all inhibitions and find the release that will hand me peace after the fact.

It had me under review. I was to follow up on another return just to create a challenge to help me get through. So, when I reach my pinnacle, I could skip that too. There was no condition, no repetition; just a vision to comply to next final admission. An energy that created the piece.

I was seen as easy target enough to gradually get back on track and break the cycle the system left to eradicate and teach me a lesson to get me back on track. I was seen as an easy target and left to pick up where I left off. It affected me at every angle and faced me with a feast.

I had to embrace that case, convince my spirit otherwise so

when I reach my pinnacle, I could present the corrupt with a condition that will resemble the ten commencements. A command to unravel the truth. For it was those inaugurations that served humanity, a moral and ethical sanctity.

I had to release, find peace, catch up with an old encounter. Because he who knew, took me in, and faced me with a credential that warned me I will never get in; nor win a thing. For I was on the edge trapped in the middle of a journey and a riddle that was nonsense it made no sense to me.

For that trend had me case close, lead the pact. Face an error and help me get back on track; all in one terror attack. I was held hostage just to get in and reap a reward from within. An energy that had me face an old game had me gamble a trial that served me a willingness; to harm me he who harmed me.

Meanwhile I get back on track and feed of the unity that served me well. It handed me the freedom to express my gratitude and extend that warranty, long enough to face another trace. It put the corrupt through exile stepping into a trend that served me well in the end.

A scheme that brought me shame, forced me to hit back. It was part of a task that was a given, a theme in between. It was part of a demonic entity in the mist of all. Trying to rise above that fall that had me waiting for the trend to break free. Handing me a trial an error to recover from; like no other.

It was part of a division that had me gain intuition. Collecting data from that mission that forced me off the edge straight into a disposition. It was part of a game that forced me to remain the same. A warning with no reservation, just a common ground, added with interrogation.

It was part of a made-up story in my head that manifested; before I had a chance to get ahead. It hit me with a curse that had me fight back and reverse. It was in a given position that forced me to hit back and face another tradition. It gave me a chance to release that demon that had me wonder.

For what it was worth, and what energy followed, it gave me step forward. a chance to sweeten the deal get back on track and state the obvious. The corrupt were feeding off me. Trying to redo and reclaim another final degree. It was forcing me to hit a blunder; a turn of events that disturbed me.

It was handing me a key that led me towards a terrible act of defiance. It had me break the silence and feed off the tremor that hit me with an extension to that redemption. It had me rehearse and follow up on a curse that served me well where the only thing that saved me broke the spell.

It served me well it brought me back to reality. Fast forwarding to the next level skipping a trace and escaping to the next race. so, when I reached my pinnacle, I could hit back face the truth and break the system that forgot to mention I was nowhere near that deviation from that manifestation.

It was facing a task that led me to embrace my truth. Where the evaluation to that challenge ended, I was stuck trying to compete with those who knew and so wanted to wrong me right through. Where the end had me denied me access where I was one that created the piece.

I was lit up, lined up, fed off by the corrupt and faced with another trilogy at the end of that unity. that forced me to release a lead up towards the next breed. Facing the corrupts final endeavour establishing the truth and releasing that demon handing no access; no longer.

For the race, caved in on my opportunity to divide conquer and develop another warning. It was giving me the impression I was nowhere near that dream that brought me here. The trend had become obsolete the treatment was incredibly wrong, and I was in terrible shape because of it.

For that journey had me face a trace, that had me convinced I was the reason the presentation was uneven. In fact, I was the one who created the piece, it brought peace after the journey was calved and halved. It had me creating a trend, that was serving me well in the end, handing me the conclusion.

I had stepped into unknown territory, torn in more than one direction. Where those who knew, were on the mend, personally attacking me under the raider again. They were trying their luck to return and attempt to hand me bad luck. All while they face me with and invasion to that manifestation.

For the interaction was not part of a manifestation. It was created by the corrupt to serve me wrong when I reached my pinnacle. It forced me to hit back with one more chance to get back on track. It was part of a follow up, based on an extinction to that prediction.

It handed me the conclusion to repeat a treat. A chance to hit back with a chaotic effect; a challenge that will serve me well at the end of that threat. I had to report, rebel against those who served me wrong. Then when the time come feed off the connection break the chain and separate every game.

Leaving the corrupt suffering all the same, it was part of a game; that restored my energy. It had me face another synergy, creating a trend that had me repeat a dead end. It was presenting me with a clue and forcing me to reclaim and face a disclaimer to game. It had me remain energised all the same.

I was in the middle torn in-between, feeding off the riddle. It served me a single serving, a challenge that was never part of the game. It was just a given response, to hit back with a trend to get me back on track and face a dead end. A mimic come to fruition, hitting me with emotional blackmail.

For those who had made it to that next level, assumed I was in it to win it. It had me face another projection to that deception. It had me case another trace, for the key was creating an expense that had me face another trace at the end of the race it had me condition the mission with a competition.

The impression set me alight, it gave me the trend that had me face a dead end. There were interruptions all around it had me face a profitable sound effect that served me well. For the service was fake and the presentation was elate. It took me on a journey and put me through hell.

It broke the spell. It gave me a second trial to return and hit back with an interaction that held me to ransom. An incantation forcing the corrupt to return for one more investigation. For those who took that interrogation as an interpretation. Handed me the opportunity to delve into that scrutiny.

It was forcing me to retaliate and break the cycle. It had me face one more fear, before I ended that trend. It was feeding off the corrupts made up story that brought me back to reality. It was part of an admission ending that impersonation. An impression handing me a final trick; to that resurrection.

I did not fall for the lie nor the impression to get by. For the deception and the invasion that served me an impromptu effect was handing the corrupt a dead end at the end of that threat. It had me force my way through, just to release that feast that encouraged me to return and find peace.

I had to break that chain, that served me the same presentation. Face another interrogation to that final manifestation, it forced me to recreate a trend that had me face a dead end. For this reason, I had to stop and feed off another creative test. A tradition that forced me to reappraise and process.

All while I get in and take what I knew and face what I thought was the last resort. For the momentum to that initiation took me on a path that had me reach my pinnacle and face that trace that served me well. It presented me with a gift that took me on journey that forced me through hell.

The trace was part of a case; it landed me a role that handed me a clue. It saw me easy and created a journey I never knew. All because the corrupt had me facing another review. It forced me off the edge straight into a method that led me to a belief. A thought that took its toll, a last resort from within.

I needed to initiate the role, face a trace, and feed off the mission. Meanwhile I repeat every competition then when the time come overcome that admission because the competition was done finished and the energy that created the piece. It had me advised ready to hit back with adversity.

It led me towards an interpretation, forcing me to repeat a follow up to the next destination. The mission was not worth my while. It had me facing a trial, that earned me a key. All I had to do was cause an effect; create a piece. State a fact, press delay, delete formulate a new improved treat.

I was on the mark, embarking on a new trend, stating a fact and trying my luck to start again. Where I get in and test the patience of those who invade and free themselves from that tight fight the one that had me stagnant to my development. I was living a chivalrous lie. trying to get by.

A trace that had me face a case warned me I was stepping into a trend that had me start again. I was trying my luck by facing my demons on the hope I feed off the energy that had me condition my mission. I had to face another competition. Then when the time come hand me a challenge.

It took me in and faced me with a trace that had me forced to hit back from within. It warned me I was on the edge. It forced me to restore my energy and pledge. It had me feed off the trial the error and the final vendetta before I hit the release button from that endeavour.

It was part of an initiative, facing a win to that inning. I had to give in break the silence and prepare myself for a step towards a direction that will hand me a final manifestation. I was to get back on track and face a trace at the end of the race. Warned of the outcome, the one that was open to investigation.

It had me on the edge; facing my true reality. A lead to a past event, it had me face another threat. It had caused an effect and had me feed off the mission after the fact. I was forced to return for one more chance to erase that case that warned me I was facing a pathway that was harming me heresy.

The road, I was on; was part of a trace, in a trance; a worthless list of demands. Where the corrupt warned me, they were watching me. It handed me the clue I needed to watch them too. Little did they know I was watching from an angle, that served me a show, a scheme in the middle of that theme.

I was handed a vision to hit back with a competition. The decision to heave at the end of that scheme served me a well-deserved and desired result. The one I needed to redeem my truth and face another reality. For the thought that gave me the power to follow up on the last resort was minimal.

It led me back towards a journey to help me get back on track. Feed off the trend push them in the corner and start again, all while I release that beast that had me face another feast. An initiative that had me face another final endeavour. A challenge that will fix it; periodically harming me like no other.

This time around I saw the light and the initiative. It was way too hard to state a fact nor even trouble me to get back on track. I could not careless, there was no connection just a deception from the statement of a fact. It was my turn to hit back and feed off the corrupts resurrection; back-to-back.

He who knew gave me an indication I had no freedom nor foundation to fight back. What I had was a presentation, to add to that manifestation. An evaluation to repeat the next follow up to a journey that will unfold had me face another trend at the end of that final test.

It was handing me the incur to break the system and feed off the mission. All because every trace had me face a case and follow up on another competition. Every journey threw me off track and forced me to fight back. It was giving me the indication the journey handed me a publication with one genre.

It forced me to face a true reality; it gave me a second chance to repeat, rebel, trap those who put me through hell. I was ganged up on; locked in against my will. I had no choice but to return hit back, rejoice, face another trace at the end of the race. Handing me the equation to fight back that invasion.

For those who put me through hell, were handed a spell. A free ride to the other side. It was giving me a point, to release that beast, fight back and hit a hold up; all in one setting. For I was given a reason to follow upon a good cause, so when I reach my peak, I could stand up for what I believed in.

Win every battle, no war to stand in my ground. For the corrupt had no power to return and devour. The poise to that served me that feast, handed me a true reality. It led me to believe the troubles had me cleared from ransom. Held up, caused an effect, served me well at every attempt; just to pitch in.

It had me in contempt, holding on to the forte. One foot

in the door the other heaving once more. Holding on to a key that led me to believe that every trace handed me the courage to return and reach my pinnacle while hitting my potential. While I watch the corrupt plumage straight into sewerage.

I was served well put through hell. It forced me to release and find peace after the fact. Giving me the power to get back on track. Where the only thing that had come to be, gave me originality to form a certain angle of a final review. Forcing the corrupt to take a gamble and fightback.

It was part of an everlasting truth, facing me to cause an effect. It had me release that beast that took me on a reserve. Handing me the motivation to step into the next destination. Forced to reclaim a new division, to a game that was testing my patience. Handing me the enclosure I needed for closure.

It was part of a publication that was pending. Faced with a clue that had been trending. Handing me a chance to face another review. I was given a challenge to break the system, in advance. A trance that was trending. All so I can skip that too, I was overtaken and surprised by the invasion.

It had me follow through to the next level. Just to a trap he who had it in for me. It led me to a destination, where every reservation forced me to outdo. I had to embrace, cause an effect, and feed off the clue. Returning the favour while I resurrect was the only way through.

I had to overtake another trace at the end of the race. For he who had to undo another review had me trapped right through. It got to the point I had no freedom to ripen; I had no trend to invade, nor invite an advert to that spite. I was to envelope a trend, because every entrapment had its own bend.

It caused an effect empowered, the truth and took over that debt. So, when I caught the corrupt reunite the return will end in tragedy where this time around, I hit the antiunity. It gave me a second chance to hit back in advance. All while I force my win, trapping those who trapped me and got in.

CHAPTER 6

◆ ◆ ◆

TIME TO UNDO RELEASE THE BEAST & SKIP THAT TOO

For all I knew and for what it was worth, the corrupt did not get through. For they were way to heaved, heavy and humbled for way to long, holding on to me as if I was their meal ticket to the next level. I was trying my hardest to harvest but all it did was fail me right through.

I was left to release the beast; stuck in the middle of a feast. So, when I reached my pinnacle, the journey would remain the same and I would fall into a trap of fading away. It was part of my truth, a challenge that will serve me well. It gave me a second chance to face a trace and feed off the case.

I was on the move; it had me creating a vision that served me a competition. I was to harm he who was in rivalry with me reviving another theme to that scheme. So, when I hit the end of my position that was in motion I would be stalling for a warning. I touched my peak with a remarkable occurrence.

I would pass that phase, hit a daze reach my pinnacle and start again. It was a viscous cycle of events that had me face a trace at the end of that trend. It had me releasing that relentless passageway. I was to undo a passion that will serve me well at every direction. A foundation that created deception.

It forced me to reveal, revive, and follow up on another dive. I fell deep into a trend, a case that stated a fact, had me reaching my summit and feeding off the threat. It became a treat that pushed me off the edge. A perception to that manifestation that had me wrapping it up with one more pledge.

Realizing I was locked in, reliving a nightmare from within; just face another cynic. Because I failed to remain silent in the mist, there was always a chance I would hit back in advance. I was taken out of my comfort zone, a temptation that became part of an invasion, handing me a conclusion.

The journey was part of an illusion, that angered me and handed me misperception. Someone was working under the raider to raid my head, face me and feed off me to get ahead. It had me follow up on a tradition that had me face a competition. It tampered with my soul and hand me confusion.

Those who used my intuition to get in, had me face a dead end from within. I could not follow up on a dream; I was too busy dramatizing in between. For what could have been, had me facing a false reality. A likely to deserve truce, a desire to break that that chain that had me face another bad day.

For that short fuse, broke the silence, handing me bad news. It was part of a clue that had me become the odd one out of that line up that used me for every trial and error a drama that served me well at every vendetta. It was part of a trace that forced me to repeat and replace.

It had me face a trauma that led me towards a journey like no other. It handed me a clue reserving the right to embrace another trace at the end of the race. A challenge that will serve me right through. Giving me an impression, I was nowhere near the corrupts interpretation, towards that vision.

An identity crisis had me on a ledge, pledging to be heard. Climbing every step, had me reach my pinnacle, hitting a threat. Where every trace had me face a case. giving me the impression once again. I had no freedom nor foundation to project nor pretend. My journey was too hard to comprehend.

I could not set a goal, create a piece, long enough to set it free. I had to let it grow gradually. It was presenting the corrupt with a debt. A challenge that will give me the power to rebuild and free myself from that old skill. It was creating a challenge that will serve me well; a test that will put me through.

All so I can continue to no longer dwell. It was troubling my soul about to relive a drama that fed off me whole. I was living proof; in between the dream and the stim in between. It had me lead the pact and scheme, while I create a challenge that had me step into a journey that unravelled me.

For what it was worth, there was no trace nor trouble to face. It was part of a given, a last respite between the old the new and what was to come; after I fell into the deep. For all I knew the dream became a drama and the only thing that served me well from within; was the key to the next revision.

I was conversing with the two, just to get through. I had to follow up on a challenge that had me fight a lost cause; it had me feeding off the trauma that had me face another trace, at the end of the race. I felt overwhelmed trapped in the middle of a profound outlook, waiting for the corrupt to outdo me.

A trace in the end, had me stepping into the unknown. I was torn in two directions revived ready to disclaim and remain alive. The event had me hit a dead end, a trapped by those who knew so I no longer had to pretend to help them get through. For that case had me face another trace.

I thought, it was part of the last resort, it had become part of a vision of skipping another scheme. It had streaming for events that had me face an indifference at the end of that trend that forced me to disclaim another dead-end. I had to feed off the energy that stated the obvious and served me well.

It was part of a cause of action, a challenge that handed me an abreaction. It was to help the corrupt face another trace giving me a chance to enter the energy that served me well at the end of that malarkey. It handed me the drama that served me a well from within.

It had me creative, leading me towards a journey that was charming. I could sense a warning in the mist. Where I hit a threat, challenged it and handed the opponent a debt.

It caused an effect and broke the system so I can claim another deception to that redemption.

It had me follow-up on another mission waiting for the corrupt to hit a competition. It was part of a trace that was never meant to be in key. For the traumatic event had me feeding off the trace that broke me and my system at the end of the race. It was part of a trick that served me well at the end.

For that forthcoming spell reminded me there was no trend worth the troubles because the end result was not as alarming as I thought there were to many energies wanting to become enemies. Trapping me in the end and leading me to a destination where the corrupt lose all power and reservation.

I no longer had the strength to pretend; it gave me a trap I needed to comprehend. What I knew and what was true, had me face an informal investigation. A task that had me refine the mission to convey and convince the corrupt otherwise. It was one bad decision, handing me one hell of a competition.

I was on the mend, trapped in the middle of a dead end. I had to refine, follow up on a trace, just to hand the corrupt a chance to return reveal and replace. I was on the edge, waiting for it all to blow over; only to witness I hit an eyewitness. Their intention had given me the impression; I hit an invasion.

The concept had ended long ago; it had me on the edge; stepping into a pledge. On the go trapped in the middle of a dead end. A trace that had me repeat a trend. I had to catch up and face a conspiracy that locked me in. Handing me an intention to break the silence from that fake interpretation.

For the energy, that had me face the corrupt, caused an effect and handed me an emotional blackmail. It led me towards a journey where the energy to release that beast became second best to that method that had me return to convey and confess. I was on the edge trying to pledge a scheme.

A trace that saw me easy warned me there was no trap that forced me to reveal nor revive another trace at the end of that trend. For I wanted to sacrifice my soul and harm he who harmed me. I was left to release that beast that served me a feast handing me an experiment to that extension.

I was earning no points; I was left to recreate a challenge; It took me on a journey that will save me at the end of that retreat; that had me start fresh and press delete. I was in the middle of a second trial. Seen as a loser, a liar, and a troublemaker. Left to retaliate as I tolerate another drama in-between.

Every time I hit an ending the corrupt were surrendering. It had me step into a trap, that served me unwell; it handed me an entrance that put me through hell. The curse had me rehearse, relapse and then come first holding on to that thirst. The one thing that had me trapped from within; warned me.

I was left to suffer in silence hitting an alliance forcing my way through. It had me define another energy that forced me to repeat replace; what I assumed was the end of the race; all while I press delete delay and follow up on another gambler along the way.

I was given a chance to report what I knew and free myself from a journey that served me the wrong right through. In the end of that trend, it had me start again. It forced me to react irrationally just to find peace from that dead end. For every time I hit a trace it turned out to be a crime.

I come out the other end in trouble again; it gave me a chance to override what I thought was the last resort. So, when I hit the end of that trend the travesty that followed through had me regain conscious awareness again. Forced to hit a hold up ready to repeat and face another cover up.

I had to entrap that trend that handed me hit a dead end. For the corrupt were on the move, it had me recreate a challenge that had me face a trance at the end of that trend; that had me start again. I was sorting out the old creating a new line of treasure; all so I can return for another measure.

A chance to return and belt the corrupt in advance praised me. I had to encounter another revelation to that manifestation. Served well at every confirmation, stepping into the indefinite feeding of revelation. It forced my way in create a new win return the favour and pretend I had no freedom.

I had to complain, then comprehend what angle I should take. All so I do not lose the game, because the game was set up by the corrupt. I had no freedom to release no challenge to find peace and the only thing that served me well from within; was a trend that had me face a dead end.

The challenges I faced were embraced by the case. It embarrassed the corrupts method, handing me an evaluation to that combination key, a stolen entity. It had me on the edge preparing me for another pledge. I had to force my way in, create a new win, feeding of the drama while stating new sin.

Served well from within. I had to face my fear and relive a trace at the end of the race. So, when the time come break the cycle and the system from within; releasing that demon that forced me in. I had to face another trace, to that case that caused an effect. It finalised my method so I can resurrect.

I had to reach my pinnacle, not allow the way in, to become the everlasting doubt from within. Feed off the drama all while the rest repeat. Then replace, what I assumed was the end of that commune. Try my best to acclaim a given a momentum to accompany me freely, towards the next test.

I had to return the favour feed off the trend; then without fail start again. It handed me a second trial, a social experiment that led me toward a new improved journey. A jealous outcome that forced me off the edge straight into a vision a challenge that will hand out a final composition.

A tool to remind myself I hit the end of that travesty. Entertained by the old, created by the new feeding off the energy that had me face a clue. It handed me a challenge that forced me to return for another yearning. In the end I had to start again and wait for the corrupt to release the beast.

I was on the edge, prolific, staling no longer, preparing for one more pledge. Repeating a new trace, that gave me a second chance to restore my energy in advance. I had to replace the old, start new and face an evaluation to that accommodation that served me well right through.

It handed me an ongoing restoration to that accommodation. I was left to release, enter the corrupts feast. A realm that will entertain them with the same crown. So, when I reached my pinnacle, I could enjoy my endowment. Then entrap another trace catch up and feed off the corrupts faith.

A final test that will fail them, at the end of that conquest. It was handing them an entrance that will stand the test of time, an end to that spell. One that was forming an alliance, for he who knew was told to return and screw me right through. An expense that will hit the end of that trend periodically.

I was on that path, for one reason and that was to reach my pinnacle and make my mark. It had me returning to repeat another storm in a new improved form. Because I was on the go, I hit an entrance to that no show. Warned once more, that I was on a path less likely for me to stand my ground.

It had me create a piece; make it happen and release the beast; all in one setting. I hit an encore once more, an uncanny trace. That made the test of time, even harder to process. One thing that stood to be true, was I looking the same and waiting for the corrupt to return to repeat another game.

I was hit with the same game, the one that had me on the edge, gambling that dream. It was not set in stone in fact it was created by an emotion in-between here there and everywhere. It was my way off accepting defeat allowing the drama to unfold, handing me joy, resilience, and passion.

It had me stand strong, return and press replay all while I resonate and feed off the trace. It had me give in and replace another case. So, when I catch up, I can repeat clear my name and press delete. All so I can cause an effect, pause; then resurrect from that threat that served me a debt.

Turning the corrupt against each other was my way of accepting the worst. Because they caused such an effect a harsh reality had given me the impression I hit a deception from a failed resurrection. I was taught a lesson and left to repeat holding the forte at every theme.

Waiting for my road to recover from that severity; became personal. I was stuck living in a time warp, once again reliving a nightmare, fighting for my life. All because the light that was handed to me was artificial. There was no trace, I was trapped in the middle of a race.

The passageway towards the tunnel, had no return. The exit was nowhere to be seen, there was no extension, just a final resurrection from that redemption. Served well, when I entered, there was no trace no case I could come and go as I pleased. The entrance was the exit, an easy way out I assumed.

In fact, it was part of the game that was giving the corrupt a chance to rise above that trance. All so I can remain the same. I was in total ore with idea; little did I know the thought would take over and I would be stuck reliving a nightmare again. The trace became a trend that had me face a dead-end.

I had no freedom nor friendship to absorb. It was all prewritten, left for me to relive another traumatic event. It had me stepping in to the unknown; forced to hit back with remorse. Not knowing where I was heading ad if I would make it to the next level. I was stalling long enough to prove my theory.

But the hard truth was not going to set me free. There was a journey I had to get through, handed me a triumph. A dead-end challenge that was to give the corrupt a chance to develop as they divide conquer and advance. All so I can get in catch up skip that trend that served me well in the end.

For I was given a chance to hit back in advance. A challenge that saw me through, also handed me the vision to investigate that interrogation. So, I can get in catch up face a final case and condition the mission, feeding off the manifestation. For every time I did, I would be stuck in a trance creating a loss.

For that task was part of the corrupts final key. the one they needed to harm me. It was part of a will of a testament. It handed me a clue, caused an effect, and created a challenge. It was trapping the corrupt with the energy to face them with a failed enigma. A trace that presented me with a feast.

I was put through hell just to give the corrupt a chance to unravel another conundrum. It was handing them release at every revival and hunting me down at every survival. Repeating what I thought was the last resort. I was given a challenge that led towards a journey so far.

So, when I reached my peak I could stand my ground, solid and sound. Waiting for the right moment to repeat face another trace and hit that clue that had me feeding off the allegation that served me an investigation. Warning me there was no trace just a given theme to break the silence in-between.

It was all part of a given, where the light of the moon; became my retreat from that loss. The part that had me rise above and beyond. There was no truth in the matter because the resurrection was an allegation from a past redemption. It took me on a path that had me redeem another scheme.

Warning me the drama was too hard to face a trend. It was part of a key that had me repeat a report. Handing me an artificial restoration, to the next vile investigation. A trace that was to stand time; an easy way to carry through. All because I was seen as an easy target; by those who were victims too.

CHAPTER 7

◆ ◆ ◆

A THEME THAT BECAME A SCHEME IN-BETWEEN

> *I was taught a lesson, left to repeat and return for another scheme in-between. For that deception became an illusion to the corrupts resolution. I was living in restitution, trying to claim another condition to that repetition. I was left unmarked report and repeat another trace to that case.*

It had me repeating another rise; above the occasion and under the raider. I was hitting a hold up, because the mission was corrupt. A test that took its toll it, had me face another trace at the end of the race. I was on the edge restoring my energy at every motivation.

It became part of a trend, that gave the corrupt a chance to pretend. I then hit a hold up, where it led them to a dead end leaving them suffering in silence while I continue on my journey, restoring my energy once again. It was feeding off the trace, that lined me up for a key at the end of that anomaly.

It had me replace the old, with the new; an urge to return for another clue. For I was given a trace to end a trend, a warning that was harming my thoughts in the end. The response was part of a given it trapped me in-between. Handing me the forbidden, a thought process that had me recreate a need.

I had to follow up trap the corrupt force my way in; succeed and break the silence as I reprieve. It was part of a pointless affair, that served me well, when I hit the end of that spell. A destination that was branding me handed me an extension to that redemption. Forcing me off the edge of salvation.

I had to face a trace, hitting the end of that trend; trapped once again. I was living a nightmare so I can start fresh. Yet again, stuck in the middle of a dead end. Trying my hardest to harvest as I continue to repeat a reward and present me with a challenge that had me stagnant to my development.

The lesson lived and learnt; was burnt. The only way I could release and find peace was face that beast. It was part of a test time for their patience ran thin and I was ready to pass another test from within. While I point the finger to, he who had me hinder. It was a reminder I was warned way to early.

Having me hitting back with surly, was the corrupts way to delay. All so they can get a chance to hit back in advance. It had me repeating another curse to that verse. It took me straight into a brand-new pledge, trying my hardest to harvest and free myself from that debt that handed me a death threat.

All while they compete complete another task and continue to repeat another seam. Where the unjust loose that reach hit the end of the pinnacle with no pledge no preach just a dead-end at the end of that trend. Meanwhile I press delete delay restart fresh and regain my conscious awareness again.

For every momentum had me facing another warning. Where I stood to be free from that anomaly. Where the trend became final and my faith in the end presented me with a dead-end. Feeding off the concept while I continue to recharge and change my revenue, using the corrupt as profit.

I was on the move, restoring my energy at every synergy. I hit common ground repetitively waiting for the corrupt to return for one more chance to hit me in advance. That repertoire took me on a journey that had me questioning the motivation of he who knew and he who had a clue.

It served me well and forced me to recreate a challenge that took me in and prevented me from repeating a new creative sense of serenity from within. I was taught a lesson left to release forced my way in and face another feast. I was trapped in the middle, forced to hit back and face another impact.

The corrupt had me stepping in to a rhythm, facing another trend in the end. It had me forced to hit back from within. I was fed off from an angle that held me up and left me to hit back with an enigma at the end of that trend. The case was torn, in two sworn it will break me and the corrupt will yearn.

For the desire to hit me and run became part of an expense. It was part of an enforcement that served me wrong in the long run. So, when I hit the end of that trend, I was hitting a dead end. Warned of what was to come from that chaotic event. It handed me a clue and presented with a point of view.

I was handed a reservation to that motivation. It warned of what was to come from that manifestation. For all I knew there was no trace no trouble no given because the journey was Humble. I was left to return repeat a new treat, trap those who remember and recreate a trend that will make them forget.

It had me rebuild and restart a presentation; that handed me faith. It warned me there was a given reason to hit me with treason. A foundation to break the system handing the corrupt a dangerous momentum one that will hand me a key facing me with a true reality.

All I had to do was haunt the corrupt and face them with a trial and error at the end of that tremor. A trace that will serve them well at the end of race. That was I had no love Faith or Hope in Humanity what I had was a dream. A challenge to evoke that demon from within.

I had to make a difference and the only way I could was redo that revue. I was to partake that clue and force the corrupt off the edge, all so I can ship that out to who knew and to he who had a clue. For I hit more than one direction harming me at every emission.

Where the opportunity to hand the corrupt rejection created cohesion. It was part of a deep understanding, that ended when I hit that hold up. Having me sinking in a sorrow, full of a foolish game a sin that had me remain the same. An effect that was trapping those who used me.

It was purely to claim another chain reaction. A trend that was no part of that rejection, it was part of a redemption that handed me the rude awakening. It handed me the evaluation to sit back and face another return; from that manifestation that served me well.

It forced me off the edge, I had to regain conscious awareness again. It was giving me the hope I had to reach my potential and face another trace. No foundation nor the freedom to hit back with treason. It was handing me validation giving me the vibe to step into a trace and face a case, out of line.

The hardship that led me to the next level had me pending. A trend that had me fail and start again. I was trapped, served an overlap, so when I hit the end of that trend; it served me a dead end. Giving the corrupt a chance to see I had no freedom nor foundation to break the system.

A deep and meaningful feeling that come over me. Where I had nowhere to turn and no freedom to repeat. For I had come to the realization, that every foundation handed me the evaluation to prepare the corrupt for a final revelation. I hit another scheme because the corrupt saw me easy.

They wanted a piece of me, and instead of creating a piece, where we could balance with a united front. They came after me in droves, trying there hardest to harvest, around my vision. Leaving me suffering in silence. As if my mission did not matter and those who knew had me locked in; powerless.

I had no fear, just faith in what I knew, because my experience taught me well. For what I knew had me relentless, I was trying my hardest to review another overview. It had me face another fear follow up on a feast and retrieve the end of that challenge that had me heave.

Forcing my way in and breaking the cycle from within was entertaining. I fell into a proposition that served me well. There was a trace that had me challenged an energy that had me overcome another outcome. It caused an effect and had me return all while I catch up and face another resurrection.

It was part of a trace that had me rewarded, giving the corrupt a chance to hit back in advance. An everlasting approach; part of a dramatic effect. Facing another failed attempt; I was to catch a break. Break the chain cut the cord and start again. It was all part of a trend that was pending.

It had me face a dead-end, a challenge that served me well in the end. For that trace became part of an endeavour. A given factor that changed my perception and handed me an extension that became part of my redemption. It was an entrance to an era that was forbidden; not forgotten.

Before I had a chance to redeem myself and follow up on a scheme. There were several on my raider trying there hardest; to come forth and repeat after me. The fact the assumption was not part of the admission I was given a chance to release a vision to that competition; that forced me off the edge.

It gave me a chance to release the beast; forced me off the edge. Trapped in the middle of a pledge. It took me on a journey, less likely for me to prevail. A hint was served, and I stuck in the middle of a faith that had me resting in my reality. A notion the corrupt were certain, they hit me with a potion.

It created a challenge that had me forced to hit back with remorse. Observing what I thought was part of a riddle. It had me condition the mission, releasing that decision and delegating what I thought it was part of a competition. It was a given, to release all inhibition; trapping those who knew.

For those who had a clue, left to redeem that theme, embracing another scheme. It took me on a journey warning me there was no given reason, just a step into what I thought was the wrong direction. In fact, it was my right to evaluate, accentuate and hand me the energy to rejuvenate.

I was living proof, that the two worlds were cut and I hit an in-between. It was just a warning; to allow me to break the trace that had me face another case. It had me waiting for the curse to come first so I can return the favour. All while I rehearse, reversing it back to the sender three-fold.

For the energy that served me well had me reveal what I knew. It created the energy that was failing me right through. It was handing me the concept; I needed to claim my truth. Because every challenge had me revive, force me inwards and created a journey that served me well from within.

I was over the redemption; there was no recovery the dream had become a drama, and I had lost the freedom to recreate a better understanding at the end of that trend that had me face a dead end. For the energy that faced me had forced me to return for another turn.

It gave me the impression I hit a hold up and the only way I could get in was press replay. It had me face another trend in the end. It was starting to look as if I was renewing another trace at the end of the race. It was part of a renewed effort, to catch up and feed off the corrupt.

I had to reclaim another division and gamble the corrupts competition. Just to force my way in and finalise that ending that had me reliving another rude awakening. For the case was encouraging me to repeat and restore my energy interrupting the corrupt at every final remedy.

For the game had me troubled, it became a silent adventure. It had followed me at every stepping stone. It was part of a trace that caused an effect and handed me the resolution that forced me off the edge. I hit a hold up a given a reason to reclaim and provide the corrupt with a brand-new game.

I was on the move preventing the corrupt from returning for another yearning. I was on the cusp preventing the unjust from arching me up. They had me locked in, forced to hit back while the corrupt pushed me off track. I had to face another trace, track down those who added to my problem.

It had me feeding off the game, and reach my potential regain conscious awareness again. I was forced towards a contest, follow up on a conquest. A given momentum took its time, belted with an insecurity with in. It pushed me off track, targeting those who knew, marketing there method right through.

They could not wait to enter my realm, solemnly entering my spirit somehow. I had to find a way out of that doubt, by screwing those who knew and follow up on those who had a clue. It had me face another avenue, forcing me to rise above and beyond feeding off the concept so I can remain strong.

In fact, it gave me the power to own it; sacrifice those who sustain it. For the energy to fight back with unity, was unidentified, it became interrogation that had me terrified; then in turn forfeited. Because those who knew added scrutiny to my journey. Just to hand those who had a clue a sense of reality.

I had to release and find peace after the fact. It forced me to enter and find a way to repeat repel and reward myself somehow. It had me on the edge delaying the truth, forcing my way through because those who knew were trying their luck to fight me back and hand me bad luck.

I had to face the facts right through, allow the corrupt to return and second guess me. All while denying them access. For my destiny was prewritten, not by those who knew nor by those who had a clue but the journey I was on created a trace to prove my theory right through.

For the method was interrogating me. It had me unravelling the truth, where it took me a moment to witness that every foundation handed me an eyewitness. There was no testimony, no progression to that manifestation; just a method praised by those who had a clue.

A generation gap, that served me well right through, stepping into a rude awakening. It gave me a second chance to follow up on a review. It forced me to rise above and beyond, feeding off a well-served concept. It had me face an upcoming case. A challenge I had to praise, attacking the method.

It left me restrained, stringing the corrupt along, trying to create a challenge to write a wrong. For the outcome to keep up with the program became a step forward. It had me working towards a rising star. Risen towards a direction that handed me the manifestation, towards a journey; that led me onwards.

Towards a journey that served me well and presented me with an upstaged spell. A trace that had me forced to remain strong, a choice that served me well and handed me a forthcoming spell. It had me face another imperishable event. I was on the move, simple and single heartedly trying to compel.

For every chance I had, gave me a choice to rehearse reverse and rejoice to the last choice. It had me forced to cause effects. I was given an entrance to return for a second coming. I was turned ready to hit back with a final feast. I had calm down feed off the turn of events that served me well.

I had to compete and face another hell forsaken spell. I had to review then face the truth, for each concept had me stir the pot handing me ending I needed cover up another step towards a direction that served me a resurrection. All so I can comprehend another dead end in the end.

I was taken for a ride reached my pinnacle and forced my way in. All knowing I hit a dead end from that trend. It was part of a spell that warned me I was off with a bearing. Staring up at the ceiling a vision of complicity no more. Just a challenge that had me face another trace, at the end of the race.

For what was to come from that malicious outcome. A vicious circle, a cycle that had me face another trace. A vision that took me on a journey that served me; God Willing. It had me forced to hit back with remorse; a challenge that served me well. It broke the silence while I was put through hell.

I had to reminisce, and force my way in. Every trace became a quest and have me face another test. For that contest was based on a downfall from within. A given momentum that served me serenity. It handed me the trace that forced me through, causing an effect and feeding off the defect.

I had no choice but to preach my truth trap those who advocate on a lie to get through. The hint had hit a hold up at the end of the race. Handing me a clue, one by one, holding me to contempt. It had me face the energy, I was not expecting. For the trace became invalid and the case extended.

It had gotten to the point I had no freedom to follow up on or a given reason to hit back with treason; until the corrupt confessed there was no time out just a follow up to a feast. I give in break the silence, from within trapping those who used me get in. Then face me as if they will win everything.

I decided to refine, repeat, and push he who knew to his limits. Feeding him what he needed to hear, just to get through. So, I can follow up on another clue, it had me serve the corrupt another dime then serves me a relative number of dead ends. So, I never claim nor reach my pinnacle again.

It had me give in, relate refine and follow up on a trend that had me face another dead end. Just to catch up and catch the corrupt about to sin and laugh at me again. I hit a funny feeling and revealed piece to that feast that had me challenge the corrupts method; to help me find peace.

It had come to my attention I had to rise above that redemption. become part of an abnormal reality. A normal response after the fact, for every time there was hell to pay the corrupt will return and hit me with a trend. Serving me well restarting my energy rebuilding a new improved accrued clue.

CHAPTER 8

◆ ◆ ◆

STEPPING INTO THE UNKNOWN

I was in the middle of making it happen; a second trail, created by peace. I was reliving a nightmare, ignoring the drama that was about to unfold. A challenge that had me reprieve, follow up on a skill feed off the trace that had me relive a tradition; stepping into the unknown was my admission.

I walked into a second trial, no longer in denial. Releasing that presentation prepared the corrupt for a resurrection. It had me trapping those who were in denial, assuming watching my every move will hand them a second chance to dive into my interest and create a piece to reserve a feast.

There was a trend, that was pending and a trap to trick me in the end. Where every follow up had me face a dead end. I had to trace that trap, trick those who knew and create a war in my spirit to get through. The traumatic event caused an effect; there was no trace nor tradition in that threat.

It was just an admiration, to that destination it led me to repeat and rebel against those who put me through hell. I had to follow up on a key, then trap those who used me to get in. Warning them from within the troubles that faced me forced me to regain conscious awareness again.

I was on the move, trapping those who endeavour to repeat and devour. Assuming they had power in numbers to create a war in my peace. But what they had handed me a clue it created an expense that had me reach my pinnacle and face me with a dead end and death threat in the end.

There was a chance for me to create an anomaly in advance. Just to get a follow up on another feast. I was pressed for time, left to repeat a trace at the end of the race. A trap to overlap and create a tradition to get back on track, became a positive affair. It handed the corrupt a dead end in the end.

For that everlasting preach was forming an alliance. It was handing me a dead end at every defiance. That mission had me interacting with an intruder; that was interfering in my vision. That is when I knew I was on the move; attached to something new. A curse that become creative served me well.

The only way to keep the flame from burning through, was hit back run and hide; from those who knew. I had no choice the corrupt were on my case, advising others how to release that feast. Force me off the edge so they can find peace. I had to warn myself on a contingence diving into a vengeance.

I had to face a conspiracy that had me on the edge. I could not fight back nor pledge because those who knew threw me off the raider by stabbing me in the back. It left me for dead, so they can get back on track and face another thread. A second trail that will hand me denial from that turn of events.

That interpretation presented me with an investigation; paused an effect. It had me stepping into a stagnant affair, straight into a trend. I was forced off the edge, repeating a truth to that truce, surrendering. I had no choice I had to fight back, irritate those who needed me to get back on track.

Warning me I hit an expense that was yearning for my existence. I was on the move, trapping those who knew and warning those who had a clue to return and not give in. For those who knew were using those who had a clue to get through. Torn in more than one direction forcing me to restore my energy.

There I was again trapped in the middle of a dead end. Where I was given the opportunity to hit back with scrutiny. I had to repeat and face another condition at the end of the mission. Thoroughly looking from within, waiting for the corrupt to discern. While I follow up on a trace that had me invalid.

I had to invade in the corrupts final revivification to the next destination. I was fighting for my life entering the unknown facing another scripture to that rapture. that served me well at the end of that forthcoming spell. Trying to release that beast, that had me rewind back to that feast.

I was taught a lesson warned of that redemption. It caused an effect and wrapped me up in a final web. It was part of a reserved attack, handing me the relation I needed to step forward and get back on track. I walked into that manifestation that haunted me, at every thread of redemption.

In the end, the race became part of a trend. It had me face an attempt to start again, where if I did not tread carefully or give in to early, I would fail immensely. I decided to reclaim my truth catch up on an old wound, hit back, and face an impact to that one track mind a vision overload the divine.

Leading up to where I was, had me face an appreciation, changing my destination. It was handing me the evaluation and a need to return for validation. I needed to spray venom, break the cycle and the system then release a trace at the end of the race. As I continue to lift and face a drift from that draft.

As I find peace get back on track; feed off that release. A trace that served me well at the end of that spell; hit just before I hit an encore. For he who harmed me, alarmed many. Followed me until the end, a decision to keep up with the program was disturbing me; it forced me to return for a yearning.

So, when I hit the end of that trend the energy that created the piece started again. I had to release peace, all while handing me the invasion; to create a better equation. It was part of an extension to that redemption. Where that entrance had a downfall, handing me a fault.

For I was given a reason to rebel against those who create treason. For what it worth, there was no trace worth the troubles no faith less taken and a follow-up to the next destination. I got in fed off the system, created a vision, and prepared myself for a trend at the end of that scene.

I was served well in-between it was meant to be part of a hard truth. A kind way of accepting that the invasion to manifestation was nowhere near that condition that served me a compelling competition. It had come to my attention, was nothing but a trap from a true cruel reality.

I was living a lie to get by; I was fighting for my life because those who knew could not wait to state a fact and fight me right through. It had me face another impact to that trace that served me well at the end of the race. I was stuck in a world where it unfolded and everything fake false no longer moulded.

I was stuck in a false review, trying to get out of a debt; that had me face another threat. I was torn in more than one direction, feeding of that manifestation. A trace that was trending and a temperance that was never-ending. A social encounter where they will sacrifice a soul, handing me the enclosure.

I was given the opportunity to survive on scrutiny, then when the trace became part of the game it gave me a second chance to rewind back to a trend that served me well in the end. It was part of an energy to feed off me whole, leave me suffering in silence; so, the rest can continue to roam.

It forced me to renew contaminate he who had a clue. It faced me and left me worried because the way I was treated was misled and I was overloaded with regret. The trend became vile the choice became part of a game, that had me on the edge, surrendering at every pledge.

It had me in the middle of an intricate detail; a complexity that left me second trial. It was all about the syndicate that created an irate amount of stagnant energy. I was surrounded by negativity death threats dead ends and a constant reminder; I was not welcome anywhere.

I was handing informative content, worldwide; it was

Golden. Those who were final were interrogating me handing me denial. It gave those who had purpose, a reason to passionately hit me treason. It had me on the edge, observed by my case, leading me towards a destination that turned heads.

It reserved me the right to declare and disclaim another division to a game that had me on the urge. I was interpreting that everlasting trend at the end of that trace. It served me well and presented me with ongoing spell. It gave me something to think about. For the challenge was based on past secrets.

They were using me to get through, assuming the method will hand them a challenge to break the system. Where the cycle and the trace that had me face a trial. It forced me to release that beast and face another trace. So, when I caught up, I could undo that everlasting review.

They were on the run terrorising me on top of everything else. My spirit was functional my journey became part of an erratic game that served me a purpose and drove me towards a pathway of uncertainty. It had me face another failed case hitting me at every momentum.

It was part of a free ride to indulge on the other side. I fell into a dilemma that served me a vendetta. Where everyone I met had me step up, into a debt, stagnant to my development. It was as if the world had gone mad somehow; everyone I met were corrupt. Waiting for me to show up just to shut me up.

It was about to go sour, and I was left to revive another dive. Then remain lined up for another game. A journey that turned into a disastrous momentum. I was left in dire straits taught a lesson that created a challenge that served me well. It was presenting with an upcoming spell.

The one thing that had me facing a dramatic effect from within. It had me face another demon to claim my vision catch up and feed off the competition. I had become vague at every violation, trapping those who hit a dead end at the end of that destination. The only way out, was to cause an effect.

State a fact, create a feast, follow up on that revision; then hit with a passion. It was a journey less likely for me to fail; more likely for me to prevail. It was preventing the corrupt from returning and denying me access. Every time I took the road less travelled; I would have a challenge to overcome.

It was a journey to serve me well, aiming for a powerful display, of freedom along the way. For every challenge I had worked hard towards, led me on. From heaven to hell, to mind body and spirit, there were no limitations. The soul was to connect and the energy that served me well was to resurrect.

The trace was a faith less likely to eradicate, it had me face another trend, at the end of that dead end. It was part of a simplicity, back when everything was starting to look innocent again. It had me reach my price then gather the energy I needed to release that piece. Harming me at every feast.

There was always a place; in the heart of evil, for that case had me cause an effect. It had me reap a reward face a reality check to an abnormality that served me well at every forthcoming spell. Then when I least expect it add to the drama reminding me, I had no freedom nor foundation to repeat.

I had to reclaim and follow up on a clue, so when I reach my pinnacle release that demon that served me a bird's eye view. It was part of a manifestation, that led me towards another destination. It had me step into a trend that created an enigma to that stigma, in the end of that dilemma.

It forced me to repeat rebel against those who had me release that feast. It presented me with a challenge that led me to find peace. I had to fight my way through, no longer questioning what I thought was part of a conspiracy to hand me a warning. Creating a challenge that served me well.

I was torn in more than one direction, ripped to shreds at every emission. Admiring the concept from afar had me step into a deception that had me repeat every motivation. Embracing my truth had me on the urge ready and willing, God willing; to surge from that splurge.

It was trapping those who knew, creating a stigma to that enigma. It had me win a trace, reach my peak, trap those who rewind, feed off the energy that survived that lie. I had returned for a new improved unveiled thread. So, when the time come reprimand those who define my existence.

There was no time to rely on whom ever to get by. No authority to speak of the drama continued, the trace reviewed, I on the other end starting again. It was part of a hint of sorrow, caught up giving in, reach my potential and break the chain. Feeding off the trauma that had me remain silent once again.

It was a given, a chance to return and belt the corrupt in advance. A presentation, had me regain my vision; trapped in the middle of a second trial. Because the mission became part of a competition, it served me well at the end of that remission. It had me face a trace cause an effect and repeat a defect.

It gave the corrupt a chance to rise above and raid the heads of he who harmed me to get ahead. It had concluded the facts; it was part of an illusion that served me well. It brought me out of that complete confusion. It had me on the edge facing another interpretation to that manifestation.

Having them confess at every deception made me feel a sense of security. Not only I was on the mend from that trend, but the corrupt return for a dead end. A trace that had me repeat rebel and force me to restore my energy all by feeding off the concept that took me through hell.

It forced me to return for a review. I was on the other end repeating a new theme. A trace that had me on the edge scheming with those who used me to get in. The assumption I was their meal ticket to the next level. It was a key for to release that beast that forced me to kindly state a fact.

It had me facing the facts, with a reality check at the end of that pact. I was outnumbered, and untamed, I felt like an outsider trying to get in the game. In fact, I was the one who created that piece; I had all the answers written in my head then on paper burning every page so I can get ahead.

As if it was a challenge to create a service where my light that lit, had been dimmed. For everyone I met briefly became a debt and a death threat. Those who were part of the threat took me in and prepared me for a challenge from within. It had me face a trend that served me well from that warning.

It led me off the bend, straight into a dead end. It caused an effect, handing the corrupt a chance to return and resurrect. I had to win every fight just to prove I was being stalked. I gave in and gave the corrupt a chance to get in and win a fight. All so I can trace it and follow up on a given base.

In the end of the case, it had me facing a raid to that dead end; it had me pretend. It was lining the corrupt up for a final vendetta, a dead end at the end of that trend. It warned me I had nowhere to go nothing to show and nowhere to be heard for those were harsh; had to many hangups.

Because they had to stir the pot, I had to back up and create havoc, at the end of that trend. It forced me to reveal and revive a dive to the corrupts finally. I could not undo, state a fact, redo, nor replace a follow up on another clue. For what it was worth, it had nothing to do with morals and ethics.

It was something else, I could not explain. It was creating a sinister effect, a dramatic entrance from a past deception. it was as if a demonic entity entered wanting to feed off the drama section by section. It was part of a dirty trick, I had to replace, while I follow up on another case.

I had to face a trend at the end. The journey was part of a trial an error and a failed attempt to feed off the tremor. It made me see there was no activity that had me feed off the creativity. It was not worth the rumours. I was not going to lose my life, just to hand the corrupt a chance to redeem itself.

I had to get back on track and attempt to feed off the trace that handed me a terrible act of kindness. It had me face a trip down memory lane and follow up on a journey all the same. It had me forced to hit back with an advantage that served me an entitlement. Just to look forward to another force.

I had to look out and fast forward to the next, not look back and face another trace. For I was not that advanced, if anything it had me repeat and follow up on a trend in the end. It was part of a trend that had me forced to hit back with remorse. A review that served me well and had me face another skill.

It took me on a journey that served me well. It was part of a curse that trapped me, a challenge so I can be averse to the next curse. A given reason to release that beast and feed off that tradition that had me on the repeating another competition. It forced me off the edge stronger than ever.

It had me pledging my truth. It was part of a trace, that had me fast forward and skip it all. An ending that was pending and trip down memory lane that was never ending. It was unravelling the truth handing me the turn of events I needed to get back on track and vent.

All so I can rise above that fall, it had me glorified once and for all. Where I challenge the corrupt from within then Give in and feed off the method that served me well. I was to catch up and torture who to get through; only God knew. All I knew I had to face another reserved activity to that severity.

It was part of a safety issue, where I get in and return the favour from within. For that scrutiny was nowhere near it was meant to be because I hit the end of that travesty. One that will corrupt the corrupt and hand them vicious cycle of events. Just to see the tradition unfold and the story be told.

CHAPTER 9

♦ ♦ ♦

WHEN THE EVENTS UNFOLD TURNING TABLES

I was torn in more than one direction, causing effects and facing another interference. It trapped me in the middle of a debt and a dead end. Only to realize I was not the one in debt and the dead end was not mine to live by. I was left to pick where I left off for everyone, I met; were not genuine.

Every challenge that come my way had me mesmerised, while I rise then fall. Scheming to return and belt the corrupt once and for all. There was always a journey to imply by it was part of a simple lie, that turned tables. It became way too personal; trapped in the middle of a terminal.

Where the only thing to come from that win, was cave in on the concept and create a war in he who harmed me and return for an encore. For the trace was not part of a given, for it was not what I was expecting. It was a non-win situation, where I was torn in every validation.

It became part of an erratic sentinel, to that terminal. For they returned and forced their way in, hitting back with a survival technique. Where I get in and face another tradition to that mission. It handed me a proposal a challenge that served me well at the end of that forthcoming spell.

I had to get back on track, feeding off the impact all while I fight back. Harming those who knew and facing those who had a clue. It was handing them a development that served me well. A traditional extension, to that expenditure served me. It was part an extension to that division from that mission.

It had me balancing, dividing and conquering every conviction to that competition. There was no final and the feast was part of an exception to that redemption. The only way I could return, and repeat was replaced it with another bad day. A demon that handed me a review and forced me off the edge.

It had me on the straight and narrow. Put in a position worse than I could imagine, it handed me an evaluation to that destination. It had me pause an effect and trap me at every risen defect. It was part of a keynote where I get in and break that system from within.

Leading the corrupt to a destination that will hand me an evaluation. Stop those who knew from getting through, repeating the same old game. It gave me an opportunity to create a barrier between the certainty of sanctity. For those who had a clue, were internally attacked by those who knew.

Making sure every trace, had no definition to the mission. Unless I was handed an evaluation, for the need to extend that extremity and undo that method; that had devalued me. A destination that forced me to release the beast. It caused an effect and faced me with a burnt out, from that curative event.

There were no trap and every momentum. I had no faith to erase. Because the journey was too hard to replace. It had me face another season, then return and face the music again. The method that forced me to redo, had me replace a condition, reveal the mission and create a war in that disposition.

All while I continue on my mission, warning me I had to repeat an old wound. I was to catch up and face the corrupts final written warning; then when the time come return for ride to the other side. For the corrupt were returning for a consumption to that repetition will bring forth competition.

I was on the edge, raising awareness and creating a new pledge. It was part of a trace that was running fiercely on a time belt; to the everlasting stealth standing. It will force me undo another review, conditioning the mission and feeding off the competition so I can get through.

It had me return for another mission, restoring my energy at every deception. I was left to refine and follow up on another key before they returned for another yearning. For the competition was based on a past deniable response to a challenge that had me face another trend at the end of that bend.

A challenge that took me in and faced me from within. A deception that warned me the resurrection was a lie. I had to give it my best shot, for the next breed, because they were in line to break my spirit in between. It was a fighting chance to return and face another trace at the end of the race.

It handed me the restoration that forced me off the edge, straight into a conviction I could not define nor defend just pretend. Because I was in the middle of a test, it broke the chain, caused an effect and drove the corrupt insane. It was part of a tradition ending the mission solemnly swearing.

Where the corrupt took me for a decided what my destiny should be like. The prediction to that mission was way to inclusive and I become a victim that decision. It left me humble hunting down those who were sustaining every trace. Assuming I was their victim at the end of the race.

I had to find my truth, work within my means try my luck and feed off the corrupt. It was well past that trend for that mission became a dead end. It had me pledge, creating a challenge that held me up and left me to repeat a trial. It taught me a lesson, I had to fight back, feeding off the mission.

It served me well at every competition stepping into the unknown and facing another trace at the end of the race. I was hit at the end of that tradition because the competition was not part of the vision. It was part of a trace that handed me incantation to follow upon another intervention.

It was part of an invention that was to hand me a way out. Just to give the corrupt a chance to give up, it was part of a trace that had me refine at the end of the race handing me a curse I could not reverse. It had me restoring my energy and feeding off the synergy.

Every time I hit an ending, it gave me a second chance.

Without reasonable doubt I was stuck in a journey that forced me to return and feed off the trauma; return and face a happy ending. Another trace at the end of the race. A reasonable doubt that forced me to reclaim another division.

For the game was imperishable and the trace incredibly wrong. It gave me a second chance to return and face the corrupt with a dead end. It was a challenge in the end that gave me the freedom and the foundation to pretend. Because the test I was handed was already branded; it threw me off track.

It had me face it way late, because I got in on my merits and hard work. I made my mark and fed off the corrupt from within. Waiting for them to get in and win another inning. Only to witness I had no time for that too, the trace had become part of a race, ending in my favour.

For once I got in and was given a chance to line the corrupt up for another trace. Where in the end of the race there would be hell to pay if the corrupt attempt to return and harm me again. It led me on and left me to remain silent from that trace; it had me face another case.

Where I was given a reason to break the cycle and feed off the competition. It handed me an informal stealth. A small wealth, that will bring me forth and create a journey that will bring forth peace at the end of that feast. It is part of an energy that had me stand my ground.

It was part of another trace, that made me out to be a victim at the end of that race. It forced me to regain conscious awareness again and prepare myself for a true rude awakening. For that crowd lined me up for one more review. It had me chase that challenge and stirred the pot that served me well.

It got me through at the end of that trend, feeding off that trap. I was hit at the end of that wrap. It had me face a trace, following it through to the next challenge. For the corrupt had me stepping into a journey. It led me to release that feast, that forced me off the edge, straight into a burn.

A trace became exploited, by the train of thought. For what it is was worth the presentation had me face a case; that had me fear the worst. Just so I can catch up come first and feed off the corrupt. It had me release that beast that forced me off the edge. Straight into a warning, that caused an effect.

It gave me freedom and brock the train of thought; that served me a yearning. It had me face my fear return for another trail, trace that case at the end of the race. A given reason to follow up on a condition that will break the system and fake another wrong move a tradition that hit ground up.

It had me feed off the corrupt at every recital, no trial to speak of. It had me face another outlook, all so I can catch up and feed off the trace, that had me prepared for one more scare. I had to skip that trip while I escape that pain that served me wrong when I hit the end of that melody.

It held me back led me to face another faith less likely for me to hit back and erase. For the truth and dare had become part of a journey had me prepared for one more challenge and that was to repeat and feed off the energy that handed me reasonable doubt. A road that had me face another abode.

It will bring me down, brave than ever; stronger than

before. It forced me off the edge straight into a delay. It presented me with an omen that had me break the system all the way. It served me a siren added with a silent treatment. So, when I reached my peak, I could undo sweeten the deal.

It took me in, forced me to hit back from within, all while I break the system. It served me a final ordeal a trace that gave me a chance to hit back in advance. For their level of education was based on friction not a methodical equation. For the decision to face me at every proposition was undeniable.

It gave me a chance to see everyone I met; locked me in with an inquisition to that proposition. It was my way to enter that realm feed off the trace that served me well. It was a gamble but worth that treasure that sweetened the deal and forced me to release that beast that had me face another feast.

It was the only way I could press replay and trap those who entrapped me. I had to face a challenge that handed me a treasure and a chase. Where I get through that scrutiny that had me aligned for one more trend. A task that had me hit a dead end. All so I can reveal the corrupts intention, all the way.

While I was wording it my way, warning the corrupt to stay away. The drama became a second coming it had me second guessing. Where every trace had me face another given presentation at the end of that manifestation. At the end of that request, I found myself hitting a terrible test.

It had me repeat a follow up on another quest, just to find peace after the fact. For I was left to give in, face another win and prepare myself for an ending that was pending. It had me face another test hit back with a request. Then force my way in and repeat what I thought was the last resort.

It had me face what thought will hand me the key, a challenge I needed to reclaim my destiny. It was ending and I was hitting a trace that was forthcoming. I was returning to redeem my truth, catch up and find my way through. Leading the pact and serving the corrupt a dead end at the end of that trend.

I was debating what end will make me break and what trace will hand me the interim at the end of the race. Where I was given a reason to hit back with treason, trapping those who knew and feeding off those who caused an effect, decelerating the system breaking their vision and starting fresh.

It left me wording things wrong, remaining way to level-headed. It had me giving into those who were winning. For the trace was serving the corrupt a challenge, at the end of that trend. Because I was in the midst of deleting another trip down memory lane it had me remain silent to the game.

I was on the mend, trying my hardest to harvest and follow up on a given momentum. Where I had to reframe my soul from reaching the end of that trend. It served me well; it solved every issue in the cusp of that vile affair. Every thought took me on a journey; rise above and beyond scrutiny.

In the end of the race, I was given a reason to hit back with treason stepping into the unknown warned of what was to come from that outcome. It gave me a warning at every momentum. Serving me well at the end of that spell. It had me face a trace that took me in and fed off me from within.

It had me hounding that momentum; at every whim. It failed me from within, leading me to a destination that every challenge had me served another trail at the end of that service. For everyone who wanted to play wanted to teach me a lesson all the way.

It forced me to review, fight back and screw he who knew. All while attempting to claim my truth, skip that trend that served me well in the end. Where every journey handed me a reservation and every truth caused an effect broke the system. The silence of the lambs helped me resurrect from that debt.

It led me towards a death threat, a dead end and a mythical adventure that had me start again. If I did one thing wrong, it would have given me the reason to hit back with treason. So, I decided to please them by making it happen; on the condition I could them oust them out and feed off the mission.

For those who were meant to help me turned against me. Not only did they feed off me, but they made me mean; absolutely terrifying. As if I was hired to please them, handing them interrogation to that manifestation to trouble me at every final destination. I was on their raider trying to succeed.

Handing them what they needed to breed, breath and continue on their journey scrutinising me. It had me waiting to catch up and hand them a trend to give them a challenge to serve them well in the end. What a difference a day made when I returned and pressed replay.

It brought back memories; certain things had come out in the open. Whatever come my way had me facing another bad day. It had me caving in on the concept, trapping those who knew and those who had a clue. It caved in on me; it had me on the edge sacrificing my soul and starting fresh.

I was ravenous, trying for as long as I could remember, I had to claim my truth. It had me feed off the challenge and hand the corrupt a chance to face another trace. It created an entrance to an energy that served me well. It had me facing a challenge I could not repel.

I had to return and face another trace, at the end of the race. All because every choice I made handed the corrupt a dead end in the end, forcing me to pretend once again. For every forthcoming spell, reminded me I was hitting a challenge that served me well.

I could not remember the last time I went through it all, just to repeat another adventure. It had me face another trace overcome an outcome and give in to he who knew and wanted to face me by attempting to screw me right through. How harsh the corrupt hit when they were caught red handed.

I was on the move, ready to fight back and face another trace, at the end of the race. Where I was stuck in the middle of a forthcoming event. It was hitting a dead end and a trend that had been wasted because they were hitting on a continuous basis. Waiting for the right moment to face another trace.

I was on the edge, hitting a trace at the end of the race. It caused an effect waiting for the corrupt to stall and restore their energy once again. Every trace became a case, every follow up had me engage in a séance; just to get an answer. A complexity that handed me a challenge that served me well.

For those who had spirit took a challenge and handed me a cheap shot. It forced me to erase that trend at the end of that warning. It had me regain conscious awareness again.

It had me living as if I was lady luck and everyone who met me were to hand me bad luck. While I give in and hand the corrupt a trace a trial an error and a final vendetta. It had me face a dream a second chance to belt the corrupt in-between. for everyone I met were stagnant to their development.

I was torn in more than one direction; there were several on my raider. Warning me there was no trouble just a challenge that had undone unaware and a trace that served me well, at the end of that spell. Others were not giving in and those who spoke to their spirit; were considered ill hearted.

Brocken beyond repair, crazy; somewhat energised by spirit that was dirty. Just to get a glimpse at a future trip, a challenge down memory lane. A trend that will surely drive the corrupt back to where they created it. In the end I saw the truth, so did those who were waiting; for it all to come to fruition.

I felt the drama unfold and the trace dissolve with an upcoming memory. It became a second coming. I had finalised that trend that served me well at the end of that trace. It caused an effect and brought me back to reality because apparently, I was nowhere near that terrible lie that served me wrong.

For what I thought was the last resort was the beginning of a new venture. A trace that served me well and handed me a chance to cause an effect, broke the silence. I had my last say I resurrected to the corrupts final. An upcoming event where I got in and upstaged them from within, facing a threat.

CHAPTER 10

◆ ◆ ◆

TIME LET IT GO, SET IT FREE & DROP THE BOMB

The premonition I had, was vivid; the vision was clear. The trace was stagnant, and the trend become part of an enigma. It was handing me the energy, and the entertainment to fast-forward to the next final degree. A challenge that will serve me, handing me what I thought was the last resort.

I needed to release that demon, that forced me off the edge. I was to change my vision claim my indifference and restart again, then return to rebuild fast forward and fight back what I thought was the last resort. It created a challenge to get back on track a trace to get back what is owed to me.

I fell straight into a dream to reclaim a nightmare, a division in between. It had come to my fruition that the journey hit my intuition. It gave me a trace that served me the unwillingness to erase. I was hit with a lie trapped in the middle of a trend to help me get in. Find my way through that loophole.

The only thing that served me well was the theory behind it. An energy that saw me easy; it put me through hell. Warning me, the punishment the corrupt were about to endure was pure. It was part of a pointless affair that had me facing a trauma. It had me leading the pact just to get back on track.

It was part of a key a challenge that saw me easy. A personal vendetta that had me working against the odds. It was my way of creating a piece that had me face a trace, at the end of the race. It had me way to heavy warned of what was to come from that yearning.

I was served a worry, forced to repeat regain conscious awareness and press delete. I was carrying a burden that was holding me hostage; I could not let it go unless I gave in and became a victim to the corrupts vision again. It was part of an expense that served me a task; that had me face a dead end.

It was well worth the wait; it forced me to trace trap; condition the mission. As I catchup and feed off the admiration. It had me facing a testimonial to that vision a composition that served me a willingness to break the silence. A challenge that had me see, I was nowhere near I was meant to be.

They created a journey just to cave in, catch the corrupt about to break me and burn me from within. All so they can get by, forcing me to face a trace and a death threat in between the case. Seen as I was not harmed by anyone at a physical sense. I was torn, tormented in a harsh reality; so, I harm myself.

So, when they took me in, it forced me to reveal another win. Where I had to come to terms with what I thought was the last resort. In fact, it was causing an effect trapping the corrupt in the middle of that debt. For the beginning of an ending had been pending and I was brave enough to return.

I had cleared the debt; by playing the adherent. Little did I know I was walking into a dangerous path. A way out, to regain conscious awareness and face another trace at the end of the race. It was forcing the corrupt to return and finalise that trend, that hit me with another reoccurrence in the end.

It had me preparing for a feast that served me an alliance at the end of that piece. It was forcing me to reveal and revive another troubled thought, in the back on my mind. For every time I had my faith returning, someone will come in and relentlessly try their luck to break my spirit from within.

I had to face what I thought was a written warning. In fact, it was the corrupt returning for another yearning. Trying to get my attention, by facing me with redemption. For they needed me here, to get to the next level. I was not interested; I had no faith in their revival what was on offer; was a nonentity.

They were damn praised by the trend not the trace. They were vultures, starving for independence using me as their remedy to get through. It got to the point there was no trace no challenge no tree, just a solid seed that was not nurtured. It was left to breath without the nourishment to succeed.

They were apparently told a lie, sold their soul to the devil to get by. I was taught a lesson to solve it and get through forced to restore and feed off the encore once more. For using me to get by, became so defiant, they were served a summons to hand me a reliant deficiency, to that forceful event.

It had hit me with remorse, a challenge to come forth, where I get in and face that demon from within. It forced me to catch up and break that dependency they had on me. Pushing them in the corner so they never see. It was one method yet to come to fruition but a karmic reaction to a forceful deception.

It became a challenge where I could not break the cycle, nor breath without having to step into break-in between. The journey was harmed by those who were led to believe the lie will set them free. Yet there was no set date the trace was a case it gave me permission to step into a revision.

It helped them get by and led them back to me handing me a lie. They were torn in turmoil, targeting me with vision just to face another competition. It forced me to retaliate create a first and last presentation to that destination that took me on a journey of restoration from that redemption.

All I wanted was peace and all I was handed had me wrapped up ready to fight back and hit the corrupt. What a dead end in the end, for I was led to believe a lie got in and fed off the trace that had me get in and break the system from within. All because I led them on fed them well, while I remained strong.

Handing me the evaluation to return for a faith less likely to be dedicated. For my hard work became undeniably the same past test I was left to repeat refine another deniable taste a test that had me face another trace at the end of the race. Because he who knew were cursing me right through.

I had to face another trace release that feast that forced me off the edge unable to return and pledge. It had me hit the end of that trend where I had followed up on a new trial and error in the end. Where every warning had me facing another establishment, it created an extension that had them whinge.

They tried to win me over at the end of that trend. All it did was create a trace, to trap those who erase and face me at every case. Restoring my energy, preparing for a final win. A challenge that had me fight back from within. It served me a willingness to confirm the obvious.

A faith less likely to eradicate, had come and gone it handed me a trace to serve me well and face another upcoming spell. For whatever reason I was torn and taught a lesson. It gave me a chance to return the favour and feed off the tremor. It handed me a given reason to hit back with treason.

Whomever come my way had me face another trace at the end of the day. I had to follow up on a trace that served me well at the end of the Just so I can prove my innocence all the way. As if there was unfinished business and I was the victim to an extremity that made no sense to me.

Where the only thing that served me well from within was that one thing that kept me winning another inning. It made no sense to me why I was being mistreated. Only to witness when time when by, the corrupt were using me as their cheat sheet to get in, feeding off the industry from within.

I had no reason to repeat nor report another treason. It

taught me a lesson at every invasion; it gave me a chance to hit the corrupt back at every revision, while demanding recission. Restoring my energy every time I hit the end of that trace, served me well. Ending the race sooner; no longer pretending.

It had me investing all my time and energy on the cause. It gave me a second chance to return and hit back in advance. The thought of becoming something I was not equipped to be, had me facing another anomaly. Stepping into the unknown, causing effects torn in the middle facing another debt.

So, when I reached my pinnacle, I could laugh at that debt. I was stuck with nowhere to turn nowhere to go and nothing to show. Just a final faith, less likely for me to fail and more likely for the corrupt to face me trying to steal my holy grail. It trapped me in the middle of a trend facing a dead end.

It had me question every thought that come way. For their own motivation, to debate then deplete it had me face another criteria motive, at the end of that trace that had me break the cycle and feed off the trend that served me a dynasty in the end. It had me speak my truth, without having to express it.

I had to start fresh and claim my truth, at the end of that trend. It forced me off the edge repeating a new pledge just in the nick of time; it had prepared for a warning. I had to catch up finalise the corrupt and face another trace at the end of the race. Several were on my raider trying to deny me access.

They were feeding off me at every request. It was part of a test, a trap to rely on no one thing and that was to push me off the edge so they can pledge and win every inning. It had me on the other end returning the favour hitting back like no other. A request, torn ready to rebel and finalise that spell.

I had to face another case, working against my will. For those who put me through hell were about to get a taste of their own filth. I was taught a lesson left to redeem another theme to that scheme. It was part of a release that handed me the feast torn in between he who knew and he who had a clue.

It was a faith less likely for me to repeat, and a trace that had me facing an ending; that was pending. When I hit the end, I ceased to differ I fell into a trap that failed me at every trend; that had me wither. So, when I got back on track the trend had me prim and proper.

I had to reap a reward, praise my soul for another warning. Before I hit a dead end at the end of that trend. It had me way up, close up and personal. Waiting patiently for the corrupt to end that trend. For what it was worth the last resort was the beginning of a new venture a kick start of a kindred heart.

All because whatever was said was a lie; just to give the corrupt a chance to get by. It served me wrong where I had to remain strong. Force my way in and feed off the drama that faced me when I hit the end of that tremor, facing another enigma. It served me well and fed off me while I got through hell.

It was part of a trend that served me well at the end of that spell. A tradition, that ended the mission. For the energy, that had me refrain; from losing another game, forced me off the edge straight into a curse I was to reverse but first rehearse heal then come first.

The destination had me forced, to release the beast. It was facing a reserved compilation. A complication in between, a challenge to sweeten the deal created a piece facing another ordeal. It was part of a dead end; a death trap, no trace, no achievement to praise; just a dead end.

It was part of another informative game. A challenge that broke the chain. In the end, I had no freedom from that rocky foundation to break the system; all I had was a given momentum. I had to face another addiction from that prediction. It had me feed off the admiration; that handed me faith.

It was brought to my attention; there was no assignment. I was taken for a ride, move forward and subdivide. I had to claim a transformation to that destination. Where the administration handed me secret admirers, it had me sitting pretty. Forced in the end of that cause and effect to remain silent.

In the end, the challenge ran me down and helped me run a risk. It had me on the edge restoring the corrupts energy repeating a trace at the end of the race. I was about to hit a final, then realized I hit a dead end. It had me face what I thought caused the effects, but all it did was hand me troubled.

A final decision to break the deception, reserved me the right to return. I had no reservation for that destination was part of an inverted invasion. It was handing me the entertainment I needed to repeat reclaim and follow up on another game. It had me face a final manifestation, to that contamination.

For everyone that was involved solved the issue. It gave me

a chance to divide, conquer and face another prosperity to that calamity. It had me face another chase while they achieved their goal. It got to the point I was taught a lesson and found myself in a position worse than the mission.

For what they were working towards had me facing another trace. For what it was worth they wanted to muck. It had me on the brink trapped in the middle of a scheme and a theme in-between. I had no freedom to release, no foundation to find peace, just a warning.

It had me sitting on a cloud, dreaming of what is to come and what could be, if what was to come, had become a reality. It forced me into a world of my own, seeking unrealistic goals, pausing the wrong effects. It had me releasing a demon to serve me well; so, I can resurrect.

I was led there by those who knew and wanted to harm me right through. Hitting me under the raider was the only way to get through. For I was given a reason to hit back with treason, just so I can catch up and make the corrupt see there was no unity; it was a conspiracy to harm me spiritually.

There was no challenge to overcome and a trace to erase. The energy that caused the effects was cancelled; cut to shreds. It had me face a trace, fight back and create a trend that will serve me well in the end. It had me forced to get back on track and feed off the impact.

It took me on a journey, that made me see; I was already on the go. Ready and willing to state a fact create a piece and force my way in. All while I try my luck and feed off the trace, that served the corrupt bad luck. Stirring the pot, creating a trend that will serve me well in the end.

It took me past what I thought was the last resort; it had me feed reel of that wheel, all while the rest took the initiative and trapped me in the end of that request. For I was given a reason to hit back with treason forced to release that beast that had me face another finally at the of that gnarly momentum.

What a lie I had to live by and obey, just to catch up and feed off the corrupt. For those who had me locked in had no support; What they had was the freedom to entertain me and a key to trap me. It was a challenge to overcome another era to that outcome; a journey to undo the corrupts method.

It served me well and put me through another upcoming review. It took me on a journey that saw me sweeten the deal so when the challenge undid so did he who took me in and forced me to review another clue. It saved me when I fell in and out of consciousness; it forced me to revive another dive.

For that reason, I was hit with a final trace, a given thought to hit back and face another warning. I was handed a key to he who used me to get there. So, when I reached my pinnacle, I could repeat repel and feed of the end of that anomaly. Giving he who was corrupt a final spell, ending all; finally.

For what it was worth and what was to come from that curse; it had me on the edge. It was giving me the chance to cave in on the concept and corrupt before they returned to harm me again. It forced me to release that beast and present me with a curse; that will quench my thirst.

Handing the corrupt a chance to get in and face me from within. It was my way of handing them a given, a freedom to break the system; and the foundation to rise above and beyond what was expected; before I hit the end of that trend. It took me in and faced me from within.

The one journey that served me the wisdom and the strength. It had me face another trace, cause an effect and feed off the tremor that brought me the everlasting trend in the end. It had me force my way in and feed off the treasure and the trace added with a trick in between.

The power to Plow through, had me claim another division to the game. It hit a siren, that handed me a silent treatment. I was forced to repeat, then take the initiative and press delete all because the corrupt were denying me access by delaying it all and restoring their energy so I can claim another fall.

The division to the game had me face another trend; it caused an effect and served me a dead end. It took me on a path that was to serve me a prize in the end. For that challenge had me face a trace. giving me the power and energy to embrace that trend; a task that brought me forward in the end.

I had to take a moment to release, for that challenge had me feast; off what I thought was last resort. I was given a momentum, that forced me to catch up and feed off the corrupt. It had me face, the end of that tither that served me well forcing me to hit back, erasing that failure at the end of that spell.

It put me in a position worse than the mission. A trip that served me well took me on a path down memory lane; it led me towards a journey that had me state a fact. It created a piece; forced me relay messages and face me with a trace at the end of the race. Assuming the key will hand me serenity.

It had me face a trace, gamble it all the way; just to get the entertainment needed to release report a rebound at the end of that trend. A concept that became part of a contest, that had relinquished another trace. A needed to press replay towards a game that was gospel and I was noble.

I had my faith torn, my light dimmed and the energy that I was working towards led to break the system. For what I thought was the last resort ended up becoming the beginning of a new era. I was Traced trapped from within laughed at every case. Where I was taught a valuable lesson.

I was trying to prove I was innocent, only to see I had way too many enemies wanting to break me. All because I caught them in the act of creating a final impact. I was faced with a trace; a given, led to believe that the trace was based on a case that served me a vision that forced me off the proposition.

It had me follow up on a feast, that served me well, after the fact. For the drama that stirred the pot then; handed me a test now. It forced me off the edge, straight into a stagnant affair. It warned me I was over the top, stepping into a case that had me repeat and follow up on another trace.

In the end of the race, I was taught a lesson, left to repeat another treason. It left me to embrace on a key that had me face another trace, at the end of the race. It left me hitting back, lashing out and creating a war in the piece; that served me wrong at the end of that feast.

A chance to clear the now handed me a task to free myself from that debt that had me waiting for the trace to embrace and the case to condition the mission and feed off the competition. All while I clear my name and start again. In fact, I was given an opportunity to release that beast.

Forced off the edge, straight into a pledge, facing a demon at the end of that trend. It caused an effect and taught me a lesson; it led me to believe that the dream was nothing but a trick. A trip down memory lane where every journey remained the same and every train of thought was a game.

A gamble that had me step into a true review, an evaluation that had me face a skill. A reality to serve me well right through. It had me repeat after the fact. Waiting for the corrupt to start fresh and create a test at the end of that bend. It was part of a clue that had me return the favour.

I was handed a chance to challenge he who knew and he who had a clue. For the trace served me well at the end of the race. It was a well given momentum that served me an ending that was pending. It forced me to rebuild and follow up on a new skill, so I can catch up catch a break the chain.

It had me feed off the trace that had me face a given momentum. It gave me a chance to hit back with a warning, where I was served well because the corrupt were hitting back with a challenge that broke the spell. I was on my own, where time ran thin and every drama handed me a new way in.

I was taught a lesson, left to repeat it. It created a piece, dropping that feast, a finally to that dream that had me facing a drama not worth the troubles in-between. For the corrupts chaotic event had me facing an ending that reached its peak. A feast that brought me forward served me well.

A true evaluation to my resurrection reserved me the right to condition and serve me well. Where every competition handed me an evaluation. So, when I reach my peak, I never get back up nor catch up. For leaving me stagnant to my development handed me a review that served me well.

I hit the rough and the lie became way too tough; I had enough. It was the corrupts way, entertaining for them. An opportunity to get in and face another win. Not only did I feed off the concept. But I gave it my best shot enforced my way in. I broke the silence from within, forcing the corrupt to give in.

ABOUT THE AUTHOR

Panagiota Makaronis

I studied for my Bachelor of Arts and Bachelor of Commerce majoring in Philosophy and Theology at ACU Australian Catholic University. I also have a diploma in Clinical Hypnotherapy from Sterling Institute and The Australian Academy of Hypnotic Science.

My studies included Psychology, Neurolinguistic Programming, (N.L.P). Meditation, and Spirituality. Over the years I have worked with many clients where I delved into Mediumship  Clairvoyancy Astrology Numerology Reiki and Crystal Healing.

I was on a mission of oppression, to study the human mind and see in hindsight what makes people in society click.
I was so interested in Anthropology and Sociology, I had a

lot of questions unanswered, so I decided to follow a path of the unknown to see how I can make sense of my reality.

My clients were, experimental to me. I was on a mission to investigate human nature and I met a lot of interesting people along the way.

Because I was quite accurate in my craft, I had several who became quite defensive. They could not wait to cover up their mess by challenging me, because they assumed I had a knowing, they could delete and delay me; by denying me access. All by attempting to harm my success.

That made my life quite interesting, it helped me with my writing. I had adventures, where I could sense I was on a path of defending my Honor. While others were hiding behind the truth, I was challenging it. Lucky for me I felt that I was being protected by my spirit along the way, where the Guidance from within never led me astray.

I had to take an absence of leave, because of family commitments, I went on a Sabbatical, decided to go back to university get my degree, clear my path, start fresh and bring myself back to reality.

I was fighting a lost cause, living another person's life, which lead me towards a destination where I could no longer lie to myself.

During my absence of leave, I went on a path of journalism and freelance writing, to broaden my Horizon, and to warn those who are inspired by the truth to set it all free and believe that dreams do come true.

Not only believe in yourself but in life, because life is too short, My Philosophy is not to follow others or worry about what others think neither. In the end, you have to live within yourself. Face your fears and trust your instincts. Because no one really knows what is around the corner.

No one knows unless you stick to the plan and even then,

your world can collapse, and you have to start again. I should know! I have passed several paths, where my foundation was not strong enough to hold me, and it would collapse where I would have to rebuild again.

Having said that, you must remain positive, for time does not stand still, time is of the essence. Based on how much you can achieve in one lifetime, just to leave your Legacy Behind.

I strongly believe you must follow your path and how it might look to others it should not matter. As long as you can accept who you are then anything is possible.

Where in the end, I believe the right presentation will lead you to the right destination if you persevere.

AMEN

THE THEATRICAL MELODIA OF MY LIFE : CHRONICLE ON

This book is based on my journey, the roller coaster I call life, my thought patterns, and my experiences. How I overcome so many turmoils, how I changed my perception, for it led me towards a destination that gave me tension. Where I felt I had no freedom or free will; all I had was failure.

Tetelestai Debt Paid In Full: Chronicle Xx

It is a one woman Comedy Show & I am the Comedian. I am to push forth, and preach my critical analysis. A tell-tale story, to catch up, and catch the corrupt red handed. For their mission, was to belt me to the ground. Just to hide a scam, a scheme a failed proposition in-between. A position to hand me joy, had come around.

Agrius; A Rise Above The Antichrist: Chronicle Xxi

I was on a pathway, towards a presentation, to lead me to the next destination; only to hit a hold up. An obstacle come my way; a pending trap. I remained repentant, just to get back on track.

The Iconic Door To Peace My Souls Final Feast A True Awakening

A technicality to rectify a task from the past arose. It was to bring forth peace, torn at every trace an insightful memory; I was to replace a line up, for a belting. For what the corrupt did, just to speed up the process; was priceless.

A Byway Chariot Awaits An Awakening Contingency: Chronicle 23

My Epistemology Theory, an Odyssey; My Bible! I swear by it! Where I fell into a trap and a trace that became part of a worrisome outcome.
Caught in a web of lies, taught me a lesson; left to suffer in between. Challenging another conspiracy theory, trying to prove my innocence once again.

Majestic Mysticism A Celtic Tradition: Chronicle Xv11

The Majestic Mysticism a Celtic Tradition Chronicle XV11, is the continuation of my Biblical Odyssey Series. How I survived my daily bread. A journal added by my imagination, and the extension to validate my perception. Where my mission took over my vision and created an opposition.
Whether it is a theory or an indication that I have a vivid imagination.

BOOKS BY THIS AUTHOR

The Adventures Of Ari, Stinky, Smelly & Sniffy;: A Legacy Is Born A Search For The Black Onyx Stone

The Adventures of Ari, Stinky, Smelly & Sniffy: A Legacy is Born
A Search for the Black Onyx Stone; It's Halloween, Ari is snuggled up at home with his mummy Betty, his three teddy bears Stinky, Smelly, and Sniffy, his playful kitten Uri, and his loyal puppy Pouey. While looking through an old box of photos, Ari uncovers stories from long ago of his Greek grandparents, Yia-Yia Dimitra and Papou Costa, who came to Australia on a ship called the Patris, chasing dreams of a better life.

The Adventures Of Stinky Smelly & Sniffy: A Christmas Awakening

The Adventures of Ari, Stinky, Smelly & Sniffy: A Christmas Awakening
The Search for the Ruby, Emerald & Yellow Sapphire Crystal

It's seven days before Christmas, young Ari, his mum Betty, and their beloved companions; Stinky, Smelly, Sniffy, Uri the ginger kitten, and Pouey the black-and-white puppy arrive at a charming Victorian beach house on Phillip Island. With waves crashing, penguins parading, and sunsets glowing across the veranda, the week unfolds in joyful adventures:

www.ingramcontent.com/pod-product-compliance
Lightning Source LLC
Chambersburg PA
CBHW050646160426
43194CB00010B/1829